J 576.078 Gar
Gardner, Robert, 1929-
**Genetics and evolution science fair
projects using skeletons, cere**

34028060435907
BC $26.60 ocm57202207

D0298058

5/06

BC

WITHDRAWN

Biology!
BEST
SCIENCE
PROJECTS

Genetics and Evolution Science Fair Projects

Using Skeletons, Cereal, Earthworms, and More

Robert Gardner

Enslow Publishers, Inc.

40 Industrial Road   PO Box 38
Box 398   Aldershot
Berkeley Heights, NJ 07922   Hants GU12 6BP
USA   UK

http://www.enslow.com

Copyright © 2005 by Robert Gardner

All rights reserved.

No part of this book may be reproduced by any means without the written permission of the publisher.

Library of Congress Cataloging-in-Publication Data

Gardner, Robert, 1929–
Genetics and evolution science fair projects using skeletons, cereal, earthworms, and more / Robert Gardner.
    p. cm. — (Biology! best science projects)
Includes index.
ISBN 0-7660-1175-5 (hardcover)
    1. Genetics—Experiments—Juvenile literature. 2. Evolution—Experiments—Juvenile literature. 3. Biology projects—Juvenile literature. I. Title. II. Series.
QH437.5.G368 2005
576'.078—dc22

                                                    2004028871

Printed in the United States of America

10 9 8 7 6 5 4 3 2 1

To Our Readers: We have done our best to make sure all Internet Addresses in this book were active and appropriate when we went to press. However, the author and the publisher have no control over and assume no liability for the material available on those Internet sites or on other Web sites they may link to. Any comments or suggestions can be sent by e-mail to comments@enslow.com or to the address on the back cover.

Illustration Credits: Charles Darwin, p. 29; Copyright 2003 Dick Hodgman, p. 60; Enslow Publishers, Inc., pp. 84, 92, 94; Ernst Haeckel, 1874, p. 37; Food and Agriculture Organization of the United Nations, p. 17; Jacob Katari, p. 21; Life Art image copyright 1998 Lippincott Williams & Wilkins. All rights reserved, p. 38; Michael W. Skrepnick, (composite illustrations in part / after J. Barcsay 1973, W. Ellenberger 1949, E. Goldfinger 2004, C. R. Knight 1947, P. J. Lynch 1993, E. Seton Thompson 1990, A. Szunyoghy 1996), pp. 39, 41, 62, 64, 65, 66, 122; Stephen F. Delisle, pp. 46, 78, 88, 101, 103, 109, 110, 114, 117.

Cover Images: © 2002–2004 Art Today, Inc. (finch); © Corel Corporation (earth); Hemera Technologies, Inc. (skull, peas); Michael W. Skrepnick (skeletons); Thinkstock Royalty Free Photograph (boy).

Contents

Introduction

The science projects and experiments in this book explore the many similarities and differences among living things. Similarities and differences are used to classify plants and animals into groups that share certain characteristics. The task of classifying organisms was first done by Carl von Linné (Carolus Linnaeus) during the eighteenth century. A century later, Charles Darwin developed the theory of evolution. It explained the vast variety of life and provided an explanation for the appearance of new species and the extinction of others.

Darwin based his theory on the variations that exist in living organisms. He was never able to explain the cause of variations found within a complex species such as humans. That aspect of evolution was made clear by the laws of genetics, first formulated by Gregor Mendel later in the nineteenth century.

As you read this book, your experiments will show how the genes transferred during reproduction give rise to the variations that allow species to evolve. Genes make up the chromosomes found in living cells. Today we know the chemistry of genes. They are found in DNA (deoxyribonucleic acid), a long molecule shaped much like a spiral staircase.

To do some of the projects in this book, you may need people to help you, because more than one pair of hands may be required. Try to choose helpers who are patient and who enjoy experimenting as much as you do.

As you do these projects, you will find it useful to record your ideas, notes, data, and anything you can conclude from your experiments in a notebook. In that way, you can keep track of the information you gather and the conclusions you reach. It will also allow you to refer to other experiments you've done that may be useful to you in later projects.

SCIENCE FAIRS

Some of the experiments in this book are followed by a section called Science Project Ideas. These ideas may be appropriate for a science fair. However, judges at science fairs do not reward projects or experiments that are simply copied from a book. For example, a model of a bacterial cell would probably not impress judges unless it was done in a novel or creative way. Data from experiments showing how genetic variation allows some bacteria to survive antibiotic treatments would receive far more consideration.

Science fair judges tend to reward creative thought and imagination. However, it is difficult to be creative or imaginative unless you are really interested in your project, so choose something that appeals to you. Consider, too, your own ability and the cost of materials needed for the project.

If you decide to use a project found in this book for a science fair, you will need to find ways to modify or extend it.

This should not be difficult because as you do these projects you will think of new ideas for experiments. It is these new experiments that will make excellent science fair projects because they spring from your own mind and are interesting to you.

If you decide to enter a science fair and have never done so before, you should read some of the books listed in the further reading section. The references that deal specifically with science fairs will provide plenty of helpful hints and lots of useful information that will enable you to avoid the pitfalls that sometimes plague first-time entrants. You will learn how to prepare appealing reports that include charts and graphs, how to set up and display your work, how to present your project, and how to talk to judges and visitors.

SAFETY FIRST

Most of the projects included in this book are perfectly safe. However, the following safety rules are well worth reading before you start any project.

1. Do any experiments or projects, whether from this book or of your own design, under the supervision of a science teacher or other knowledgeable adult.

2. Read all instructions carefully before proceeding with a project. If you have questions, check with your supervisor before going any further.

3. Maintain a serious attitude while conducting experiments. Fooling around can be dangerous to you and to others.

4. Wear approved safety goggles when you are doing anything that might cause injury to your eyes.

5. Do not eat or drink while experimenting.

6. Have a first-aid kit nearby while you are experimenting.

7. Do not touch a lit high-wattage bulb. Lightbulbs produce light, but they also produce heat.

Classifying Objects

Look around you. Chances are you see a great variety of things. Can any of them be grouped together because of similarities?

Grouping objects based on similarities or differences is called classification. Humans tend to classify things. You probably classify your clothes. Shirts and socks go in one drawer, sweaters in another, while pants or dresses are hung in a closet. In dictionaries words are classified alphabetically. Those beginning with the letter *a* precede those beginning with *b*, and both precede words that begin with *c*.

Part of science involves classification. Geologists classify rocks, meteorologists classify clouds and weather patterns, chemists classify elements and compounds, physicists classify atomic particles, and biologists, who play an important role in this book, classify organisms, living and dead.

Experiment 1.1

Classifying

Materials

✓ paper   ✓ pencil

Suppose you are the manager of a grocery store. Would you arrange your products alphabetically so that apples, ammonia, and animal crackers were in the same aisle? If you did, you would probably not have many customers.

Pretend that you are the manager in charge of setting up a new supermarket. Make a list of the signs you would hang over each of the twenty aisles in your store.

Because you have done such a good job, a pharmaceutical company hires you to oversee the establishment of a new pharmacy. Make a list of the signs you would hang over each of the ten aisles in the pharmacy.

Things are classified in many ways. How are books classified in a library? How are electrical resistors classified? How about lightbulbs? Pencils? Money? How about printing fonts and sizes? Shoes? Clothes?

Experiment 1.2

Classified Mail

Materials

✓ index cards
or notebook

✓ pencil
✓ lots of mail

When you send a letter, you write an address on the envelope as well as the name of the person to whom you are writing. The zip code is part of the address. The zip code is a classification system used by the U.S. Postal Service. The zip code's first five numbers are used to direct the letter to a post office in a specific city or town. For example, any letter with a zip code 06068 will be directed to the Salisbury, Connecticut, post office. Four additional digits will indicate the post office box or mailbox in which the letter is to be placed.

Most mail that reaches your home has a return address with a zip code on the upper left-hand corner of the envelope. Keep a record of the zip codes and the corresponding states and cities or towns from which all the mail you receive was sent. Use your records to determine, as best you can, the classification system used by the U.S. Postal Service to direct the mail.

BIOLOGICAL CLASSIFICATION

When you observe living organisms, you may be struck by their differences. But there are similarities too. A robin is more like a bluebird than a salamander or you. Both robins and bluebirds have wings that allow them to fly; both reproduce by laying eggs in nests; both bring food to their young until they are old enough to fend for themselves. However, robins and bluebirds differ in color, size, and many other ways, including the inability of a robin and a bluebird to mate and produce offspring.

In general, biologists classify organisms that are able to mate and reproduce as members of the same species. This means of classifying organisms is not perfect. For example, a horse and a donkey are regarded as separate species because of their differences in size, shape, and general appearance. However, horses and donkeys can mate and produce offspring, which are called mules. Mules, however, are sterile and do not reproduce.

Our present system of classifying organisms by species was devised by Carl von Linné (1707–1778). Your first and last name allow others to identify you. Linné's system is similar. It consists of two names. The first, the genus name, which is capitalized, identifies a particular group of organisms that are very similar but do not interbreed. The second, the species name, which is not capitalized, identifies a group of very similar organisms that can mate and reproduce. For uniformity, Linné chose

Latin names. (He even Latinized his own name to Carolus Linnaeus.) Your species name is *Homo sapiens*, which means "man, wise." Humans are the only living member of the genus *Homo*. However, fossils have been found that are so similar to us that they share the genus name. These include *Homo habilis*, *Homo heidelbergensis*, *Homo rudolfensis*, *Homo ergaster*, *Homo erectus*, and *Homo neanderthalensis*. The oldest of these species lived nearly two million years ago.

Linné recognized 9,000 distinct species. Today more than 1.5 million species have been identified, and there are probably millions more that have yet to be classified.

Biologists classify organisms into groups that include more and more species as they ascend the system. Just as similar species are grouped into one genus, so similar genuses are grouped into families. *Homo sapiens* belong to the family Hominidae, which all share or shared the ability to walk upright on two feet. Again, today's humans are the only living members of that family. But fossil evidence reveals that some early ancestors, such as *Australopithecus afarensis*, *Australopithecus boisei*, *Australopithecus robustus*, and others were members of the same family.

Families, in turn, are grouped into orders. Humans belong to the order Primates, one we share with apes (chimpanzees, gorillas, orangutans, and gibbons), monkeys, tree shrews, lemurs, and tarsiers. Primates have both eyes on the front of their head and possess flexible fingers and toes that can grasp objects. The top ends of these fingers and toes are covered by nails, not claws.

Orders are grouped into classes. Humans belong to the class Mammalia, the members of which are born alive and are nursed by their mother's milk. How many mammals can you name?

Mammals are all members of the subphylum Vertebrata. Vertebrates have a nerve cord that is enclosed in a series of bones (vertebrae) that make up a backbone. Thus, all classes of animals with a backbone are included in the subphylum Vertebrata—bony fish, amphibians, reptiles, and aves (birds), as well as mammals.

Vertebrates belong to the kingdom Animalia (animals). This kingdom, along with three other kingdoms—protists, fungi, and plants—falls within the domain Eukarya.

Protists are single-celled organisms. Their cells contain a nucleus surrounded by a membrane as well as specialized cell parts (organelles). You may have seen protists such as amoebas and paramecia under a microscope.

Fungi, such as molds and mushrooms, have threadlike cells that attach to and absorb food from other living or dead organisms.

The plant kingdom consists of many-celled organisms whose cells have rigid walls made of cellulose. Within their cells is an enzyme (chlorophyll) needed for photosynthesis, a process by which plants manufacture their own food by combining carbon dioxide and water using the energy in sunlight.

Members of the animal kingdom have many cells too, but their cells do not have rigid walls and they cannot make their own food. As a result, most animals have to move about in order to obtain food.

At the top of the classification system biologists have established three domains—Eukarya, Archaea, and Bacteria. Eukaryotes include the animal, plant, and fungi kingdoms, as well as protists that have cells with nuclei and organelles. (Organelles are small structures outside a cell's nucleus where important chemical reactions take place.) The Archaea and Bacteria domains contain single-celled organisms that differ in their genetic structure.

CLASSIFICATION OF SOME ANIMALS

Approximately 97 percent of all known animals are invertebrates—animals without backbones—such as mollusks, worms, insects, and crustaceans. The primary classes of the vertebrate phylum are bony fish (Osteichthyes), amphibians (Amphibia), reptiles (Reptilia), birds (Aves), and mammals (Mammalia). All the classes are egg-laying, except for most mammals, whose embryos grow within their mothers and are born live.

Members of the class Osteichthyes live in water. They respire by means of gills and have two-chambered hearts.

Amphibians have three-chambered hearts. They are usually aquatic after hatching and respire by means of gills. However, as they mature, they develop lungs, breathe air, and acquire two pairs of legs by which they are able to move on land. Reptiles hatch from eggs that have shells. They have lungs throughout life and possess four-chambered hearts, although the ventricles that pump blood out of the heart are connected by an opening in the wall between the two chambers. Birds possess feathers, which are modifications of the scales found on reptiles. Their front appendages are feathered wings that allow many of them to fly. They also respire through lungs and have a four-chambered heart without openings between the ventricles. Mammals also have lungs and four-chambered hearts. They have hair, which apparently evolved from scales.

One order within the class Mammalia, Monotremata, do lay eggs. The best known member of this order is the duck-billed platypus. Another order, the marsupials (Marsupialia), bear their young live but transfer them to a pouch, where they attach to a nipple and are nourished until they can fend for themselves. Kangaroos, opossums, and koalas are examples of marsupials.

Bats belong to the order Chiroptera. The forelimbs of these mammals have been modified into wings, enabling them to fly.

Rats, mice, squirrels, and similar mammals belong to the order Rodentia. They have chisel-like incisor teeth, no canines, and broad molars.

BALEEN WHALE

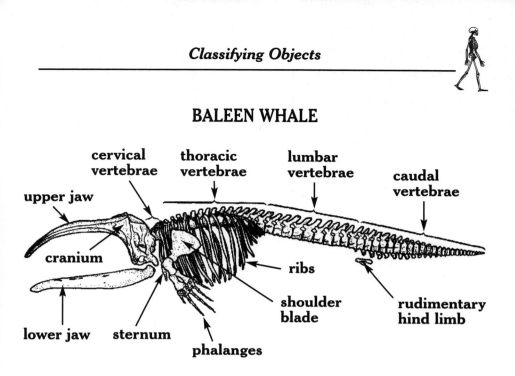

Figure 1.

Whales are mammals that live in the ocean. Their front limbs have the same bones as human arms and hands, but they have been modified into flippers. Baleen whales have rudimentary hind limbs that serve no purpose. The ancestors from whom they apparently evolved did have rear legs.

The order Carnivora includes dogs, cats, hyenas, seals, and other animals that have small incisor teeth, large canines, and premolars adapted for shearing meat. Whales (Figure 1) belong to the order Cetacea. The front limbs of these mammals have been modified into flippers. They lack rear appendages and are ocean dwelling throughout their lives. There is good evidence that Cetacea evolved from members of the order Artiodactyla—plant-eating animals with two or four toes modified into hoofs. Included are cattle, sheep, pigs, goats, camels, hippopotamuses, and other hoofed mammals.

Experiment 1.3

Classifying Some Metallic Items

Materials

✓ a variety of paper clips, nails, carpet tacks, thumbtacks, screws, nuts, bolts, wires, staples, and pins

✓ white paper

✓ a friend

Collect a variety of as many of the metallic items listed as possible. Place all of the items on sheets of white paper. Then invent a way to classify all the objects on the paper.

Which items belong to the same "species"? Which belong to the same "genus"? To the same "family"? The same "order"? The same "class"? The same "phylum"? The same "kingdom"?

From the standpoint of evolution, which objects are the oldest? (You may want to consult with your parents or grandparents before answering this question.) The most recent? Are any becoming extinct?

Have a friend classify the same objects. Then compare the two classifications. How do they differ? How are they the same?

Experiment 1.4

Classifying Animals

Materials

✓ encyclopedias and other reference materials about animals

✓ Chapter 1 of this book
✓ paper
✓ pencil

Prepare a chart similar to the one shown at the bottom of the page, which includes the common names of a few animal species (see last row of the chart). From what you have read, and from other information you can gather from encyclopedias and other sources about animals, fill in your copy of the chart so as to classify the species whose common names are given. The chart has been filled in for humans.

Domain:	Eukarya							
Kingdom:	Animal							
Phylum:	Vertebrate							
Class:	Mammal							
Order:	Primate							
Family:	Hominid							
Genus:	Homo							
Species:	sapiens							
Common name:	human	Siamese cat	German shepherd dog	Clydesdale horse	field mouse	robin	earthworm	box turtle

CLASSIFYING PLANTS

The plant kingdom can be divided into flowering and nonflowering plants. Nonflowering plants include mosses, liverworts, ferns, horsetails, and club mosses. These plants reproduce by releasing spores. Conifers, which belong to the class Gymnospermae (gymnosperms), are trees such as pines. These trees do produce seeds, but the seeds develop inside cones, not flowers, and are not surrounded by a fruit.

Flowering plants, class Angiospermae (angiosperms), have stamens that produce pollen. They also have pistils that contain ovules. Within the ovules are egg cells. Angiosperms are divided into two subclasses—dicotyledons (dicots) and monocotyledons (monocots). Dicots have two cotyledons (embryonic leaves) in their seeds, while the seeds of monocots produce seeds with a single cotyledon. There are other general differences too. The leaves of dicots usually have veins that form a network, such as the leaves of maple trees. Monocot leaves usually have parallel veins, such as the leaves of corn and grasses. The flower parts of dicots usually come in fours or fives or multiples of four or five, while monocot flower parts appear as threes or multiples of three.

The parts of a typical flower are shown in Figure 2a. The sepals are the outermost parts of a flower. They are often green and leaflike; however, in some flowers, such as tulips and lilies, the sepals are often the same color as the petals. Sepals protect

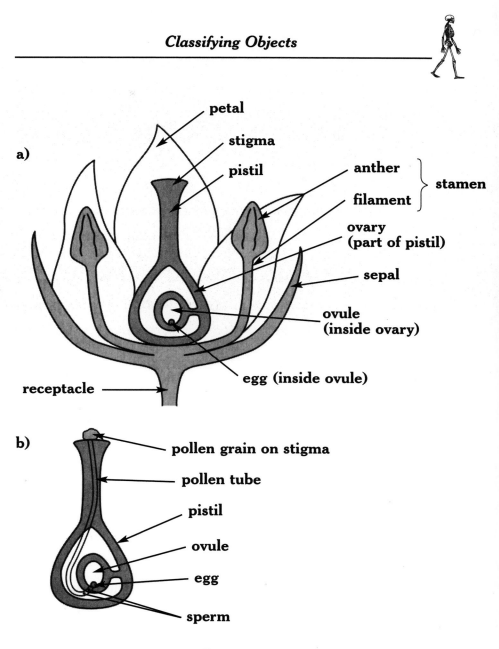

Figure 2.

a) The drawing shows the parts of a typical flower.
b) A pollen tube grows down the pistil. Sperm cells travel down the tube and fertilize the egg or eggs in the ovule at the base of the pistil.

and cover young flowers before they open. Petals are usually the bright, colorful part of a flower that lie just inside, and often between, the sepals. Sepals and petals are called the accessory parts of a flower because they are not directly involved in producing seeds.

The essential parts of the flower—pistils and stamens—are needed to produce seeds. The stamens consist of long slender filaments with little knobs at their ends called anthers. Very fine grains of pollen are found on the anthers. If you rub your finger across an anther, you may be able to see some of the fine yellow dustlike particles of pollen. Perhaps you can collect enough pollen to look at under a microscope.

The pistil or pistils, the female part(s) of a flower, are usually in the flower's center. The tip of the pistil, the stigma, has a sticky substance that helps collect pollen grains carried to the pistil by insects, wind, or water—or by gravity if the pollen comes from the same flower. A pollen grain produces a long tube through which sperm cells travel to the egg, which is located at the lower end of the pistil, as shown in Figure 2b. The union of sperm and egg produces an embryo that eventually becomes part of the seed. Flowers that receive pollen from another plant of the same species are said to be cross-pollinated. Generally, cross-pollination produces larger, healthier plants than self-pollination, in which pollen grains from a flower's stamens fall on the same flower's pistil.

Flowers that have all four flower parts—sepals, petals, stamens, and pistils—are called complete flowers. Flowers that lack one of the four parts are said to be incomplete. Some plants have flowers with either stamens or pistils but not both. Flowers with both pistils and stamens are said to be perfect. Flowers lacking either pistils or stamens are said to be imperfect. Flowers that bear only stamens are called staminate flowers. Those that bear only pistils are pistillate flowers. Dioecious plants produce imperfect flowers on separate plants. Monoecious plants bear both pistillate and staminate flowers on the same plant. The familiar tassels of a corn plant are the staminate flowers, while the silk found lower on the same plant are part of the pistillate flowers.

Experiment 1.5

A Flower to Dissect and Classify

Materials

✓ a flower such as a daffodil, lily, snapdragon, or tulip

✓ tweezers (forceps)

✓ magnifying glass

The best way to see the parts of a flower is to dissect a large one, such as a daffodil, lily, snapdragon, or tulip. If you can't find one growing at home, you may be able to obtain wilted ones free at a florist shop if you explain why you need them. Look at the whole flower before you begin dissecting. Figure 2 will help you identify its parts. The green cuplike structure that connects the flower to the stem or receptacle is the calyx. The calyx is made up of the sepals, small green leaflike structures that sometimes have the same colors as the petals that lie just above and inside them. How many sepals are there on the flower you are dissecting? Are they green?

How many petals does your flower have? Are the petals and sepals equal in number? If possible, look at the plant's leaves. Are the veins parallel or do they form a network? Do you think the flower is part of a monocot or a dicot?

Use your fingers or tweezers to carefully remove the petals. You should be able to see the stamens and pistil, or pistils, at the flower's center. How many stamens does your flower have?

How many pistils? A magnifying glass may help you see the parts more clearly. Does the number of pistils and stamens help you confirm whether the flower is part of a monocot or a dicot?

Experiment 1.6

Classifying Flowers

Materials

✓ various plants in bloom

✓ magnifying glass

✓ notebook

✓ pencil

✓ plant field guide

Examine a number of flowers, both wild and cultivated. They won't all be blooming at the same time, but you can find them from early spring until autumn. If your family grows indoor plants, or if you live in a warm climate, you can continue your search on a year-round basis.

Early in the spring, look for willows. Are their flowers complete or incomplete? Soon, other trees such as maples and oaks will bear inconspicuous flowers. Wildflowers, too, begin to bloom in early spring and continue through the summer. Look for lilacs and forsythia during the spring, as well as the colorful blossoms of fruit trees.

As you examine these flowers, a magnifying glass will be useful but not essential. Can you find the four parts common to flowers—sepals, petals, stamens, and pistils? **Be careful!** Bees and other insects will be visiting these flowers more frequently than you. Make drawings of the various flowers and their parts. Then label the parts and try to identify the plant on which they are growing. A field guide to plants will be helpful. You will find these guides in your local or school library.

Which flowers are complete flowers? Which are incomplete? How many imperfect flowers can you find? Are any from dioecious plants? Which are from monoecious plants? If you find pistillate flowers, can you find the corresponding staminate flowers? Do you find any flowers that are both imperfect and incomplete? If you do, can you identify the species?

Darwin and the Theory of Evolution

I t is often said that evolution is just a theory. But what is a scientific theory? In ordinary conversation, someone might say, "I have a theory about that," meaning a guess or a hunch. In science, a theory is much more. It is a well-developed explanation of some aspect of the natural world that is supported by a lot of evidence. During the early 1500s, Copernicus developed the heliocentric theory. It held that Earth and all the other planets orbit the sun. At that time, most people believed the sun, stars, and other planets revolved about Earth. Gradually, the heliocentric (sun-centered) theory became accepted because it provided a better explanation of what astronomers observed than did the geocentric (Earth-centered) theory. Similarly, the atomic theory, which assumes that matter is made of atoms, is currently accepted by scientists. It can explain nearly all the observations and experimental evidence that has been gathered about the behavior and structure of matter. However, there are still a few mysteries to solve, and some scientists are working to modify this theory.

The theory of evolution is accepted by most scientists because it offers the best explanation of what is now known about biology and geology. In fact, biology would be a very puzzling subject without the theory of evolution to help explain it.

CHARLES DARWIN (1809–1882) AND THE THEORY OF EVOLUTION

At the age of twenty-two, Charles Darwin was floundering. He had studied medicine and theology, but had no interest in either. Then, in 1831, despite his father's disapproval, he joined the crew of the HMS *Beagle* as an unpaid naturalist on a five-year journey. Four years later, the *Beagle* anchored off the Galápagos Islands. The Galápagos are a group of islands straddling the equator 1,000 kilometers (600 mi) west of South America. Darwin spent nearly a month there observing and collecting plants and animals. He was particularly impressed by the finches, mockingbirds, and giant tortoises. The finches resembled those he had seen in Ecuador, but they were much more diverse. While finches normally eat seeds, some in the Galápagos were eating fleshy cacti, others ate worms, some fed on insects, others on fruits. One species, the woodpecker finch, used the spine from a cactus to pry under tree bark to drive out insects. Such a niche would normally be occupied by woodpeckers, but there were none on the Galápagos. A species of finch had taken advantage of that food source. There were finches everywhere, some big, some small, some in trees, some on the ground. Interestingly, the different species had different beaks—beaks that were adapted to the kind of food they ate (see Figure 3).

Figure 3.

Darwin was struck by the differences in the beaks of the different species of finches he observed on the Galápagos Islands.

At that time, most people believed that God had created every species all at once, as stated in the Bible's Book of Genesis. But Darwin, reflecting on what he had seen, had a different theory. He believed that new species evolved over time in order to survive changing conditions. A few finches, for example, had been carried by winds from South America to the Galápagos Islands. Once there, birds on each island slowly adapted to survive on the food available to them. Birds with variations best suited for eating particular available foods survived and reproduced; those without the variations starved to death. Eventually the survivors became different from their ancestors. Over many generations, they became distinct species.

Experiment 2.1

Darwin and the Beaks of Finches

Materials

- ✓ plastic spoon, knife, and fork
- ✓ pliers with different ends (needle-nose, adjustable, and regular)
- ✓ a number of seeds of at least 6 kinds, such as thistle, sunflower, radish, carrot, lettuce, squash, and corn
- ✓ teaspoon
- ✓ tablespoon
- ✓ paper plates
- ✓ clock or watch with second hand
- ✓ a partner
- ✓ notebook
- ✓ pen or pencil
- ✓ graph paper

While on the Galápagos Islands, Darwin observed several species of finches that had never been seen before. He noticed that the beaks of each species had become modified to feed on specific foods.

In this experiment, a plastic spoon, knife, and fork, as well as pliers with different ends (needle-nose, adjustable, and regular), will represent different beaks. These "beaks" will be used to "eat" a variety of seeds.

Place a teaspoonful of each of the smaller seeds and a tablespoonful of the larger seeds in separate piles on a paper plate.

Ask a partner to use one of the "beaks" to "eat" some of each kind of seed for one minute. A seed will be considered "eaten" if it can be picked up with the "beak" and moved to a second paper plate. Each seed "eaten" is to be placed on the second plate. After one minute, count and record the number of seeds of each type that are on the second plate.

Place the seeds that were "eaten" back on the first plate. Have your partner repeat the experiment for each of the other "beaks."

After all the "beaks" have been tested, plot bar graphs such as the one in Figure 4 for each beak that was tested.

Which beak or beaks seemed best adapted for eating a particular type of seed?

Which beak seemed best adapted for eating a variety of seeds?

Were any beaks limited to eating only one kind of seed? If that seed were to become extinct, what would happen to that species?

Which seed seemed best adapted for survival?

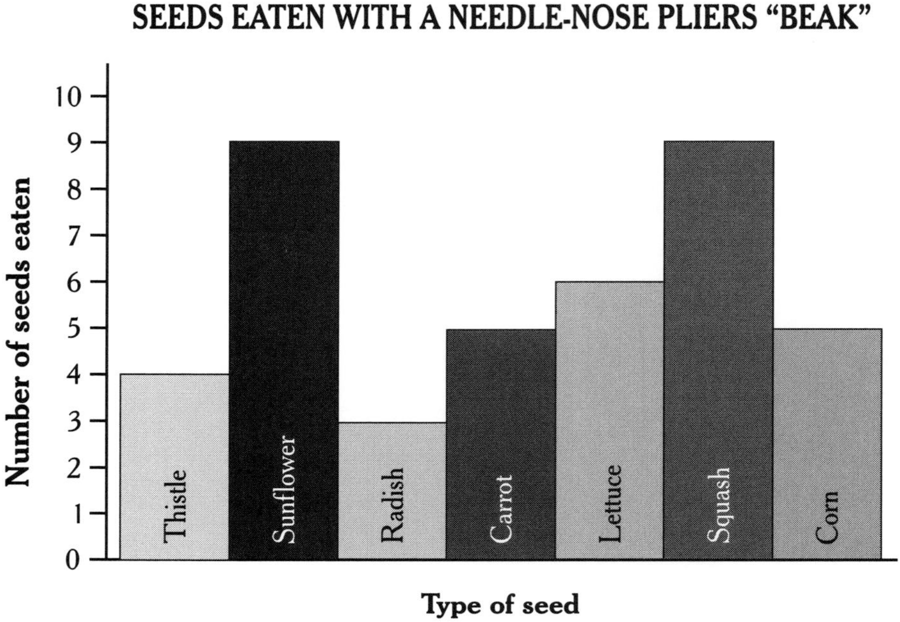

SEEDS EATEN WITH A NEEDLE-NOSE PLIERS "BEAK"

Number of seeds eaten (y-axis: 0–10)

Bars:
- Thistle: 4
- Sunflower: 9
- Radish: 3
- Carrot: 5
- Lettuce: 6
- Squash: 9
- Corn: 5

Type of seed

Figure 4.

A bar graph of the seeds "eaten" by a particular beak. Your results may be quite different.

Experiment 2.2

Seeds Across a Sea

Materials

- ✓ seawater or a salt solution
- ✓ teaspoon
- ✓ kosher salt
- ✓ graduated cylinder or metric measuring cup
- ✓ water
- ✓ bowl
- ✓ plastic wrap
- ✓ various kinds of seeds— radish, peas, cucumbers, beans, asparagus, squash, corn
- ✓ paper cups
- ✓ garden soil
- ✓ large aluminum pan
- ✓ marking pen

Darwin found plants on the Galápagos Islands that he had seen on the South American mainland. He reasoned that seeds had been carried by the wind or floated across ocean waters on driftwood or on their own until they reached the Galápagos. But could seeds survive in the ocean's salty water? He tested his hypothesis by doing experiments similar to one you can do.

The primary salt dissolved in seawater is sodium chloride, the salt you put on food. The concentration of salt in the oceans is 3.5 percent. If you live near the ocean, collect some seawater and bring it home. If you don't live near an ocean, you can make some seawater. Add about 3.5 grams (a teaspoonful) of kosher salt to 100 mL of water and stir until the salt dissolves.

Pour the salt water into a bowl. Cover the bowl loosely with plastic wrap to reduce evaporation. Add 4 or 5 seeds of several kinds to the salt water. Be sure you can recognize each seed by its size and shape. Some seeds will sink, others will float.

Leave the seeds in the water for 24 hours. While the seeds soak, fill paper cups with moist soil. Place the cups on a large aluminum pan. There should be as many cups as there are types of seed. After 24 hours, plant the seeds about 0.6 cm (0.25 in) deep in the soil. Only one kind of seed should be planted in each cup. Use a marking pen to label the cups with the name of the seed planted.

Keep the soil moist but not soggy. It may take anywhere from two days to two weeks for seeds to germinate. Did any of the seeds germinate? If so, which ones were they?

Repeat the experiment, but this time leave the seeds in the salt water for 48 hours. Can any of the seeds sprout after being in salt water for 48 hours? Can any germinate after being in salt water for three days? Can any survive a week in ocean water?

Darwin found that some seeds can germinate after a long time in ocean water. What did you find? Record your results in your science notebook.

Science Project Idea

Observe a variety of plants including trees. What mechanisms do various plants use to distribute their seeds?

EVIDENCE FOR THE THEORY OF A COMMON ANCESTOR

During the *Beagle*'s voyage, Darwin read *Principles of Geology* by Charles Lyell (1797–1875). It convinced him that Earth had undergone major geologic changes over long periods of time. If rocks can change with time, he thought, perhaps living things can also change. In fact, he knew that domesticated animals, such as dogs, chickens, pigeons, horses, and cattle, had been deliberately changed. Breeders had selected traits they wanted to transmit to the next generations. They did this by breeding those animals that possessed the traits they sought, such as speed in horses, herding instincts in dogs, or milk production in cows.

Fossils found in ancient rocks revealed that many plants and animals had become extinct. And, the older the rocks, the more primitive the fossils. Fossils of mammals were found only in more recent sediments. There seemed to be a progression of species through time. Simple organisms appear in the fossil record before more complex ones. Invertebrates appear before vertebrates; fish appear before amphibians; amphibians before reptiles; reptiles before birds; and birds prior to mammals. In addition, as Figure 5 reveals, the embryos of all animals seem very similar in their early stages of development, suggesting they may have had a common ancestor. Further, the anatomy of vertebrates shows a gradual progression from fish to mammals. And the skeletons of mammals as different as whales, bats, and humans are similar. The evidence convinced Darwin that all life had descended from a common ancestor.

Experiment 2.3

Homologous Parts

Materials

✓ **an adult**

✓ human and other skeletons (ask your science teacher or find pictures)

✓ chicken wing, cooked

✓ newspapers

✓ stove

✓ pot of water

✓ garbage bag

✓ soap and water

✓ Figures 6, 7, and 8

One example of evidence for descent from a common ancestor is the existence of homologous organs or body parts. These are parts of the anatomy that form in the same way from the same

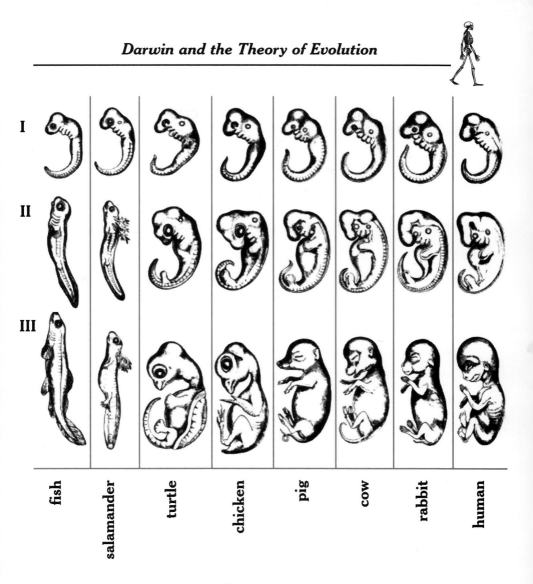

I

II

III

fish

salamander

turtle

chicken

pig

cow

rabbit

human

Figure 5.

The top row of vertebrate embryos, labeled I, are shown a few days after fertilization of an egg by a sperm. Notice how similar they are despite the fact that they develop into a range of vertebrates, from fish to humans. Embryos in the middle row are a few days older and are more distinct. Embryos in the third row are still older. They have developed to a stage that allows you to see what species they will be at birth or hatching.

tissue in embryos of different species. Although the parts are homologous, they may serve very different functions.

If possible, examine a human skeleton and the skeleton of one or more other organism. Many school science departments have a human skeleton, either real or plastic. To see a good example of homologous parts, you could examine the arm of a human skeleton and the wing of a chicken.

First, examine the arm of a human skeleton. Use Figure 6 to help you identify the humerus, ulna, radius, carpals (wrist bones), metacarpals (bones in back of hand), and phalanges (fingers).

Next, obtain a chicken wing from a meat market. **Ask an adult** to cook the wing in boiling

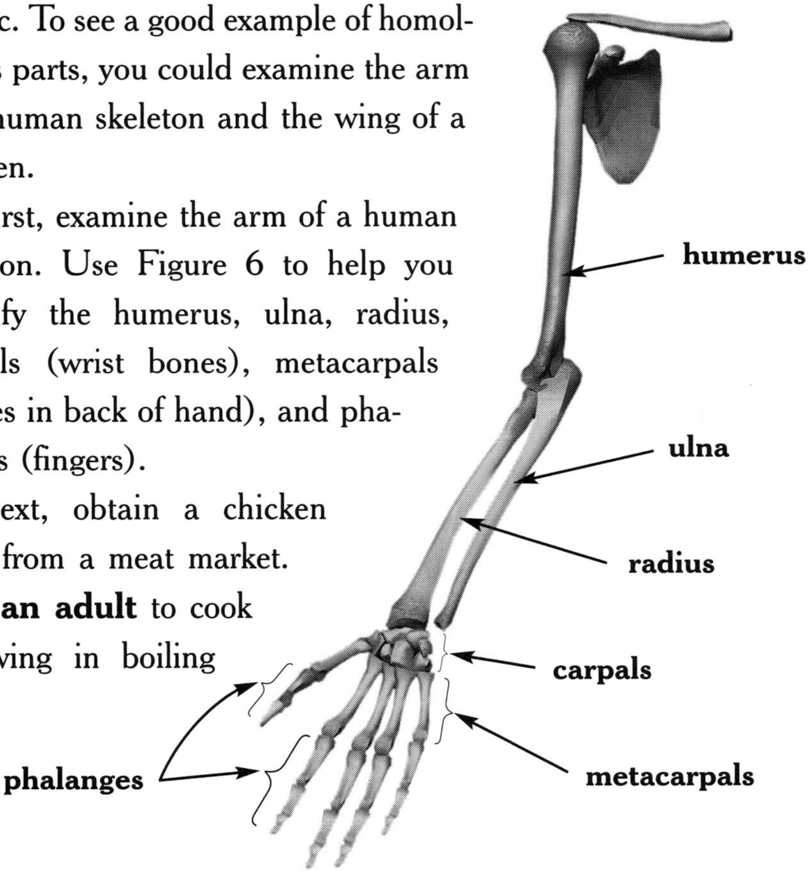

humerus

ulna

radius

carpals

metacarpals

phalanges

Figure 6.

The drawing shows the bones of the human arm. How do they compare with the bones in a bird's wing?

water. After the wing has cooled, place the wing on a thick layer of newspapers. It should be easy to pull the meat off the bones.

Notice that the major bones in the wing are very similar (homologous) to human arm bones. Can you find the humerus? Can you find the radius and ulna? How do the carpals, metacarpals, and phalanges of a chicken differ from yours? How are they similar? How, through evolution,

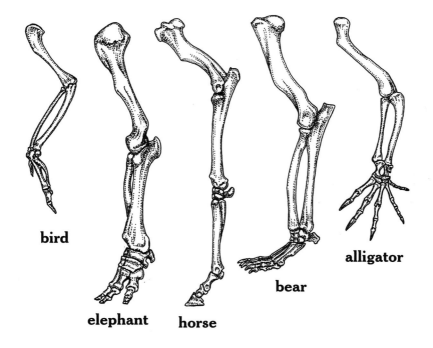

bird

alligator

elephant   horse

bear

Figure 7.

This drawing shows the front limbs of a number of vertebrates. The bones are homologous but have evolved in different ways. Notice that in some animals bones have fused. Fusion is particularly evident in horses.

have bird wings and human arms become modified for different functions?

When you have finished, roll up the newspaper around all the tissue and place it in a garbage bag. Wash your hands and all utensils thoroughly with soap and water when you have finished handling the chicken parts.

Examine the drawing of front limbs of the other animals shown in Figure 7. Identify and name the bones that are homologous to human arm bones. How, through evolution, have the front limbs of these animals become adapted for different uses?

Examine the "hand" bones of different mammals shown in Figure 8. Through time, these hands, paws, flippers, and wings have developed for different uses. But notice how similar the homologous bones of these mammals are.

Fossils revealing extinct animals seemingly ancestral to present-day animals, the anatomy and embryology of animals, and his observations during his voyage on the *Beagle* came together in Darwin's mind. The overall picture convinced him that all living things are related and share a common origin.

DARWIN AND MALTHUS

After returning to England in 1836, Darwin read *An Essay on the Principle of Population* by Thomas Malthus (1766–1834). Malthus proposed that animals reproduce faster than their food supply. As a result, population growth is eventually diminished by starvation, disease, or, among humans, war. This led Darwin to believe that variation among members of a species determines who will succeed in the struggle for survival. Those organisms best adapted (suited) to a particular niche would survive in the competition for limited food resources. And those organisms would pass on the traits that enabled them to survive to succeeding generations.

Darwin could then explain the variety of finches he had observed on the Galápagos Islands. The first finches to reach the islands would have reproduced until the food supply became limited. But some birds, as a result of their variations,

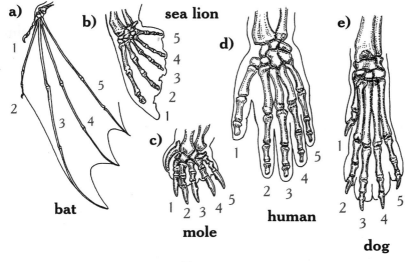

Figure 8.

As you can see, all these mammals have the same "hand" bones, but in different proportions. a) bat wing; b) sea lion flipper; c) mole paw; d) human hand; e) dog paw.

were able to feed on different seeds or a new food source, such as the fleshy tissue of a cactus or a fruit. These few birds were able to adapt to a different diet, one that most members of the species could not eat. Birds with the right variations found an untapped niche of the environment and multiplied. Eventually, they changed enough so that they could not interbreed with their ancestors and became a separate finch species.

It was the variations among the members of a species that allowed nature to select those organisms that would survive— they were the ones that could take advantage of the opportunities a particular environment offered. He called the process "natural selection" to distinguish it from the artificial selection practiced by breeders of domestic animals and plants. Natural selection, Darwin maintained, was a never-ending process in which organisms better adapted to an environment gradually replaced those that were not as well adapted for survival. Others called it "survival of the fittest." Normal variation coupled with natural selection could explain the process of evolution in which new species appeared through time as others became extinct.

Evolution is usually slow, and only examination of the fossil records provides evidence of change. Sometimes the process can be observed over a few decades. The peppered moth found in England is an example. Like all species, peppered moths vary. One variation is their color: Some are light, some are dark. At the beginning of the nineteenth century, light-colored moths were far more common than dark ones. By the twentieth century, the reverse was true, but only in urban environments. The ratio in rural regions remained the same. Why?

Biologists offered a hypothesis. The soot from the factories that arose during the industrial revolution had blackened the light-colored bark on the trunks of trees where these moths normally stopped to rest. It had also killed the white lichen that grew there. As a result, the lighter moths had become more visible to predators, while the darker moths blended into the dark background of the tree trunks.

To test their hypothesis, scientists placed light- and dark-colored moths on the trunks of trees in rural areas and in urban areas near factories. At urban sites, more of the light-colored moths were devoured by birds. In rural areas where lichen survived and tree trunks remained undarkened by soot, the dark-colored moths were the ones more frequently eaten. The experimental test of the hypothesis showed that natural selection favored dark moths in urban areas and lighter moths in rural areas.

By the middle of the twentieth century, the English Parliament passed air pollution laws that greatly reduced the soot from factories. By the end of the century, new trees with light-colored bark housing white lichen had reappeared in cities. And, sure enough, the light-colored moth population increased in urban areas and the number of darker moths declined. The moth population evolved back to the way it had been two centuries before.

Experiment 2.4

Natural Selection and Survival by Color

Materials

- ✓ sheets of green (2), white, black, red, blue, and yellow construction paper
- ✓ paper punch
- ✓ a partner
- ✓ forceps
- ✓ sheet of glossy paper
- ✓ clock or watch

In this experiment you will simulate natural selection. First, obtain sheets of green, white, black, red, blue, and yellow construction paper. Use a paper punch to prepare 30 circles from each of the six sheets of paper. Place a second sheet of green construction paper on a table. Spread the 180 circles in a random fashion all over the sheet of green paper.

Ask a friend, sibling, or parent to pretend to be a "predator," a bird perhaps, that feeds on insects on a green "lawn." The "predator" is to consider the circles as prey representing different varieties of an insect. Hand the "predator" a pair forceps and have her "feed" on the prey. Ask her to "fly" in random fashion all over the "lawn" and "feed" on the prey. Each "insect" is to be dropped on a sheet of glossy paper next to the "lawn." After two or three minutes, ask the "predator" to assume that he or she is satiated (full) and return the forceps to you.

Use the forceps to separate the circles by color into six separate groups. Then count the number of each color that the predator consumed. Which color was "eaten" most frequently? Which color was "eaten" least frequently? Which "insect" seemed best suited for survival? Can you explain how it was adapted for survival in its environment?

Experiment 2.5

Variation in Humans

Materials

✓ notebook

✓ pen or pencil

✓ human subjects

There are many variations in living things other than color. And you don't have to look far to find them. An examination of the faces, hands, tongues, and ears of a number of humans can illustrate variation. Five such variations can be seen in Figure 9.

Look at the faces and hands of different people. Some have cleft chins or dimples; others do not. There are people who can roll their tongues, but many cannot. Their earlobes may be attached or free. Some people have curved thumbs; others have straight thumbs.

a) cleft chin   b) dimples   c) tongue roller   non-roller

d) attached earlobe   free earlobe

e) straight thumb   curved thumb

Figure 9.

A few of the many variations in humans can be found in their a) chins; b) dimples; c) tongues; d) earlobes; e) thumbs.

With their permission, examine a number of people for the traits shown in Figure 9. What percentage of the people you observed had dimples? What percentage did not? How about curved and straight thumbs? Could they roll their tongues? What about their earlobes?

Do any of these traits provide an advantage to those who possess them?

Do any of these traits occur only with one of the others? For example, do all people with cleft chins have dimples? Or are these all independent traits?

Can you wiggle your ears? Some people have the muscles needed to do this. What percentage of people have these muscles? Name some animals that can move their ears. Is it advantageous for an animal to move its ears? How about humans? Why do you think some humans have the muscles that allow them to move their ears?

Science Project Ideas

- What other variable human traits can you examine? Which are rare? Do any provide an evolutionary advantage?

- Examine a litter of puppies or kittens. How do these siblings vary in color, weight, and behavior? How are they similar?

◆ At a zoo or farm, examine as many members of a single animal species as possible. What variations do you notice among these animals? How are they suited for the environment they normally inhabit?

◆ Plants also vary. You might examine corn or bean seeds. Are all the seeds the same size? By how much do they vary in size? How will you determine the size of a seed? What other variable plant structures might you investigate?

◆ What is the Moro reflex? Why might it have evolved in human infants? How did it help infants to survive? Why do you think it is still present in infants?

LAMARCK'S THEORY OF ADAPTATION

Darwin was not the first to observe that organisms change over time. As early as 1809, Jean Lamarck (1744–1829) proposed that living organisms acquire traits that help them adapt to their environment. Once acquired, he maintained, the traits are passed on to offspring. Over time a species could evolve into a form very different from its ancestors. As an example, Lamarck explained the giraffe's long neck. It was acquired, he said, because as these animals stretched their necks to reach leaves near the tops of trees, their necks became longer. Once they possessed longer necks, the trait was transmitted to their offspring. Gradually, over centuries, the giraffes acquired their long necks.

According to Darwin, both longer- and shorter-necked giraffes existed. In the struggle for survival, those with longer necks had an advantage that made them more likely to obtain food and thus produce offspring who would have long necks. Over time, animals with longer necks would prevail; those with shorter necks would not.

Lamarck's theory was discredited by a variety of experiments. In one experiment, August Weismann (1834–1914) cut off the tails of more than 1,500 mice over a span of 22 generations. In every generation, the mice were still born with tails.

Darwin summarized his theory of evolution as "descent with modification." Variations found in a species make some members better adapted for survival than others. Those better adapted are more likely to live, reproduce, and transmit their traits to the next generation. Over time, the better adapted organisms become the predominant form of the species, or they become a new species.

Experiment 2.6

World Population Trends

Materials

✓ graph paper ✓ apple or tomato
✓ pencil ✓ **an adult**
✓ ruler ✓ knife

As you have read, Darwin's thoughts about evolution were sparked when he read the first edition of Malthus's book *An Essay on the Principle of Population*, which held that organisms reproduce at a faster rate than their food supply. Another way of expressing Malthus's idea is to say that food supply increases in an arithmetic progression, while population grows in a geometric progression.

An arithmetic progression is a sequence of numbers in which a constant number is added to the preceding one, such as 1, 3, 5, 7, 9. . . . A geometric progression is a sequence of numbers in which each succeeding number has been multiplied by the same number. For example, in the sequence 1, 2, 4, 8, 16, 32 . . . , each number is multiplied by two to obtain the next one.

To understand the consequences of Malthus's idea, you can prepare a graph using axes such as those in Figure 10. The vertical axis can represent both population and food supply in separate lines with a different color. The horizontal axis represents time in, let's say, decades. Using the arithmetic progression mentioned in the previous paragraph, plot food supply vs. time. The first three values have been plotted as dots. On the same graph, use the geometric progression to plot population vs. time. The first three values have been plotted as Xes. After how many decades does population exceed food supply? What happens to the difference between food supply and population as time goes on?

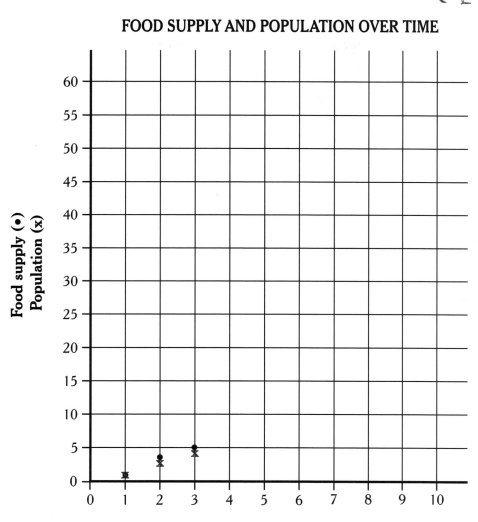

FOOD SUPPLY AND POPULATION OVER TIME

Figure 10.

Using graph paper, prepare vertical and horizontal axes like the ones shown here. Plot food supply as an arithmetic progression (such as 1, 3, 5, 7, 9 . . .) vs. time. On the same graph, plot population as a geometric progression (such as 1, 2, 4, 8, 16 . . .) vs. time.

Malthus's idea includes all living organisms. To see how it applies to plants, **ask an adult** to cut open an apple or tomato. Count the number of seeds. Assume each seed will develop into a new tree or plant. Will the apple or tomato population grow arithmetically or geometrically?

To consider a real example of population growth over time, examine the data in Table 1. It contains figures of the United Nations' estimates of the world's population from A.D. 1 to A.D. 2003. Of course, recent figures are more accurate because census taking methods have improved over time.

Use the data in Table 1 to plot a graph of world population vs. time from A.D. 1 to A.D. 2003. Starting at A.D. 1, how long did it take for the world population to double? How long did it take to double again? To double a third time? To double a fourth time?

Table 1:

WORLD POPULATION FIGURES FROM A.D. 1 TO A.D. 2003.

Year (A.D.)	Population (billions)	Year (A.D.)	Population (billions)
1	0.3	1927	2.0
1250	0.4	1960	3.0
1500	0.5	1974	4.0
1804	1.0	1987	5.0
1850	1.2	1999	6.0
1900	1.6	2003	6.3

Plot a graph of world population from 1804 to 2003. Allow space to extrapolate (extend) the graph to 2050. According to the two graphs you have made, when has the world's population grown slowest? When has it grown fastest?

To check the rate you found from the graphs, divide the population growth (the change in population from one date to the next) by the number of years during which the growth occurred. Do the numbers you obtain by these divisions agree with the answers you obtained from the graph?

How confident are you about extrapolating the graph to 2050? What do you estimate the world population will be in 2015? In 2025?

Science Project Ideas

◆ Assuming your estimate of the world's population in 2015 is accurate, by what percentage is the world's population increasing each year? At that percentage increase per year, how long will it take for the world's population to double? One way to estimate the doubling time is to use the rule of 72. According to this rule, if you divide 72 by the annual percentage increase, you will obtain the number of years for the quantity to double. For example, if the annual population increase is 10 percent, the population will double in 7.2 years $(72 \div 10 = 7.2)$.

◆ In 2000, the U.S. population was 281.4 million. Approximately what percentage of the world's people live in the United States?

◆ In 2000, the birth rate in the United States was 14.7 live births per 1,000 people; the death rate was 8.7 deaths per 1,000 people. At what rate was the U.S. population increasing in people per thousand? At what rate was it increasing in terms of percentage? At this rate, how long will it take for the U.S. population to double?

Experiment 2.7

Population Growth and a Limited Food Supply

Materials

- ✓ 4 mature earthworms
- ✓ 2 one-quart plastic containers
- ✓ peat moss
- ✓ garden soil
- ✓ dry breakfast cereal such as whole wheat flakes
- ✓ water
- ✓ cool place
- ✓ notebook
- ✓ pencil
- ✓ ruler
- ✓ graph paper

Place four mature earthworms in a 1-quart plastic container that is filled with peat moss and garden soil. Crush and grind some dry breakfast cereal such as whole wheat flakes into tiny pieces. Cover the soil with a thin layer of the cereal. Keep the soil cool and moist.

At two-week intervals, carefully remove the soil bit by bit and transfer it to another 1-quart container. As you do so, count and measure the worms, which you will then add to the soil you moved. Record all your data in a notebook.

What happens to the population over time? What happens to the size of the worms? Can you explain your results?

Plot a graph of the earthworm population vs. time in weeks or months. What is the shape of the graph? How do you explain the shape of the graph you have drawn?

Chapter 3

Missing Links, Adaptations, and Evolution Through Time

S cientists who knew Darwin urged him to publish his theory and the evidence he had accumulated to support it. But Darwin procrastinated. He knew his theory would create controversy, and he hated arguments and criticism. However, in 1858 he received a paper from Alfred Russel Wallace (1823–1913). Wallace's theory, as outlined in his paper, was nearly identical to Darwin's. Charles Lyell and Joseph Hooker (1817–1911), two scientists familiar with Darwin's work, made a wise suggestion. Wallace's paper together with a summary of Darwin's book-in-progress would be jointly presented to the Linnaean Society of London. The two papers, presented to the society in July of

1858, caused very little commotion. However, the publication of Darwin's book, *The Origin of Species*, the following year generated great controversy, as Darwin had predicted. Darwin stayed out of the fray. He let others use the evidence he had accumulated to defend his theory.

Darwin's supporters met the onslaught from some of his critics by searching for key fossils that would link modern organisms to those of the past. But before we examine their work, we should consider the vast period of time during which life has apparently evolved.

Experiment 3.1

Evolution and Time Lines

Materials

✓ long strips of paper (roll of adding machine or wrapping paper works well, as you will need strips as long as 4.5 meters, or 15 ft)   ✓ ruler

Astronomers estimate that the universe is 13.7 billion years old. Stars have been forming since about 100 million years after that, but the star we call our sun was not formed until about 4.6 billion years ago. Earth and the other planets congealed approximately 4.5 billion years ago. Until recently, the oldest known fossils were not more than 550 million years old. But in 1982 a team of paleobiologists led by J. William Schopf discovered fossilized cyanobacteria (blue-green algae) cells in western Australia. The cells were in 3.5-billion-year-old rocks. The age of the rocks were determined from the radioactive elements they contained.

Blue-green algae are able to carry on photosynthesis, the process by which green plants manufacture food. During the process, oxygen is released as a by-product. It took several billion years before there was enough oxygen in Earth's water and atmosphere to support animal life. The first animal fossils—shellfish and corals—were found in ancient rocks approximately 550 million years old.

Geologists and biologists divide Earth's history into eras, which they subdivide into periods. Table 2 summarizes this history and indicates major happenings that took place during these periods. There were apparently two mass extinctions. The oldest one marks the end of the Paleozoic era, when 80 percent of all living forms disappeared. The second occurred at the end of the Mesozoic era, when 70 percent of all species disappeared. There is good evidence that the second (and perhaps the first) mass extinction was caused by a giant meteor that struck Earth. The collision produced so much dust that it clouded the entire planet. As a result, Earth grew cold because so little sunlight passed through the atmosphere. Many cold-blooded animals, such as dinosaurs and other reptiles, were unable to survive and became extinct, as did many plants.

Table 2:
THE GEOLOGIC TIMETABLE SINCE EARTH'S ORIGIN.

Era	Period	Epoch	Years ago	Events revealed by fossil records
Cenozoic	Quaternary	Holocene	11,500 to present	Beginning of human history; climate warms after glaciers recede.
		Pleistocene	1.8 M* to 11,500	First modern humans (genus *Homo*) appear.
	Tertiary	Pliocene	5 M to 1.8 M	First humanlike (Hominid) species who walk erect.
		Miocene	24 M to 5 M	Mammals abundant; first grasslands appear.
		Oligocene	34 M to 24 M	First apes appear.
		Eocene	55 M to 34 M	First monkeys; first whales; first horses.
		Paleocene	65 M to 55 M	Primitive mammals and flowering plants abundant.
Mesozoic				Second mass extinction of living things marks end of Mesozoic era. Dinosaurs become extinct.
	Cretaceous		144 M to 65 M	First flowering plants appear.
	Jurassic		208 M to 144 M	First birds appear.
	Triassic		245 M to 208 M	First dinosaurs and primitive mammals appear.
Paleozoic				First mass extinction of living things marks end of Paleozoic era.
	Permian		286 M to 245 M	Ferns and palms appear.
	Carboniferous		360 M to 286 M	First reptiles appear.
	Devonian		408 M to 360 M	First insects appear. Later, first 4-legged animals.
	Silurian		438 M to 408 M	First land plants appear.
	Ordovician		505 M to 438 M	First fish appear.
	Cambrian		550 M to 505 M	First shellfish, trilobites, and corals.
	Precambrian		4.5 B** to 550 M	Primitive algae appear.

* M = million (1,000,000)   ** B = billion (1,000,000,000)

Among the earliest animals to appear in the fossil record were trilobites (Figure 11). Trilobites persisted throughout the Paleozoic era, but disappeared during the mass extinction at the end of the Permian period. Extinction of species is common. Scientists estimate that 99 percent of all the species that ever lived are extinct.

Starting from Earth's formation, use Table 2 to make a time line of Earth's history on a long strip of paper. If you let 1.0 cm represent one million years, how long will the strip have to be? (Remember, it takes 1,000 million to equal one billion!)

Figure 11.

Trilobites, like the fossilized one here, were abundant during the Paleozoic era.

As you have probably figured out, you would need a strip about half the length of a football field. Change the scale. Let 1 mm represent a million years. How long will the paper strip have to be now to represent Earth's entire history?

On the strip, mark the beginning and end of each era. During what fraction of Earth's history was there life on the planet? During what fraction of its history were animals on Earth?

Make another time line representing Earth's history from the beginning of the Cambrian period to the present. This time let 1.0 cm represent one million years. The table shows when various events, such as the two mass extinctions and the appearance of various life-forms, first occurred. Place these events at approximately their proper positions along the time line. How much of the time line is occupied by the genus *Homo*? By human history?

Science Project Idea

Imagine that Earth's entire history was contained in one year beginning at 12:00 A.M. on January 1. At what date and time would the first animal life appear? At what date and time would the first mammals appear? At what date and time would the genus *Homo* first appear? At what date and time would *Homo sapiens* appear?

MISSING LINKS

"If living species evolved from a common ancestor, where are the missing links?" asked Darwin's critics. Those who supported Darwin's theory began the search for what they called transitional forms. Because few skeletons are ever fossilized, the search was not easy. Although fossils are rare, transitional forms have been found for many species. *Archaeopteryx* is an example. It was a reptile, but its forelegs had become winglike and it had feathers rather than scales. It was a link between reptiles and birds. A drawing of what *Archaeopteryx* probably looked like is shown in Figure 12.

Figure 12.
This drawing shows what *Archaeopteryx* may have looked like.

Ichthyostega was the name given to a four-foot-long fossil with four primitive legs found in Greenland more than 80 years ago. The animal looked more like a fish than a land animal. It was probably the transitional form linking fish with amphibians.

From fossil evidence, scientists have deduced that whales evolved from the family of primitive hoofed mammals known as mesonychids between 65 and 35 million years ago. Mesonychids slowly evolved into *Ambulocetus*, which had paddlelike hind feet that could have been used for moving through water. Its back was flexible, so it could move its body up and down to propel itself through water just as modern whales do. A later fossil, *Rodhocetus*, probably never left the water. Its limbs were very small. It had even greater back flexibility than *Ambulocetus*. A still more recent fossil preceding modern whales was *Basilosaurus*. *Basilosaurus* had the form of a present-day whale, except for small hind limbs that were probably vestigial. That is, like the human appendix, their hind limbs served no useful function. Following *Basilosaurus* are fossils of modern baleen (Mysticeti) and toothed (Odontoceti) whales.

The transitional forms of the front leg leading to the modern horse (*Equus caballus*) are shown in Figure 13. Fossils of a much smaller animal, genus *Hyracotherium*, appeared in the Eocene period. Notice how the middle toe evolved into the present-day hoof as the other toes diminished through the Cenozoic era.

A variety of fossils leading to modern apes and humans

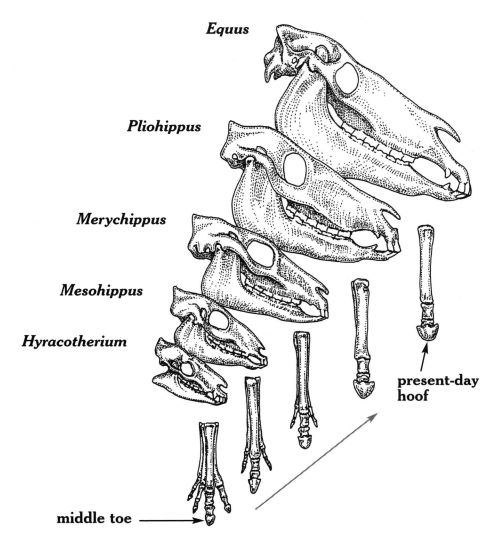

Equus

Pliohippus

Merychippus

Mesohippus

Hyracotherium

present-day
hoof

middle toe

Figure 13.

These drawings show the evolution leading to the modern
horse, *Equus*. The lower forelegs of the animals are to the
right of the reconstruction of the animals' heads. Except for
Equus, the drawings are based on fossils of these animals.

have been found. Figure 14 shows a series of skulls, reconstructed from fossils, showing transitional forms leading to present-day humans. Notice how the cranium (the upper part of the skull), which holds the brain, has increased in size. At the same time, the lower part of the face has receded so that the front of the jaw is almost directly below the forehead. What other changes do you see?

Other fossilized parts of these transitional forms leading to *Homo sapiens* show that all these species walked erect, as did a number of other early hominids. Anatomists can tell whether a species walked upright by examining a fossil's legs, pelvis, and the junction of the head with the backbone.

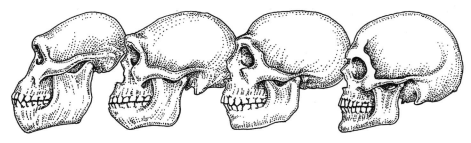

Australopithecus (3–3.6 million) **Homo neanderthalensis** (300,000–30,000)

Homo erectus (1.8 million–30,000) **Homo sapiens** (200,000–present)

Figure 14.

These drawings show reconstructions of fossil skulls. The approximate ages of the fossils (years ago) are beneath the species names.

ADAPTATIONS

Through time, the bones of some mammals have been adapted for different functions (Figure 15). Through natural selection, organisms have adapted to a variety of ecological niches. The hair characteristic of mammals appears as wool in sheep, quills in porcupines, and horns in rhinoceroses. The origin of these different structures is from the same embryonic tissue, but over time its development has been modified in different ways. These changes have enabled the animals to adapt in particular

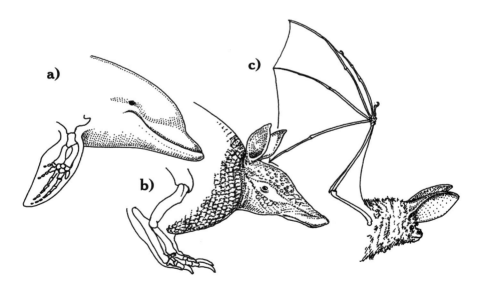

Figure 15.

The forelimb bones of these mammals have been adapted for a) swimming (dolphins); b) digging through soil (armadillos); c) flying (bats). Can you name all the bones?

ways to their environments. Although all humans belong to the species *Homo sapiens*, they, too, may have adapted to different environments.

Experiment 3.2

Adaptations

Materials

- ✓ sheets of black and white construction paper
- ✓ sunny window or a bright lightbulb
- ✓ modeling clay
- ✓ metric ruler
- ✓ notebook
- ✓ pocket calculator (optional)
- ✓ large jar

- ✓ teacup and saucer
- ✓ hot tap water
- ✓ thermometer
- ✓ a friend
- ✓ pencils
- ✓ Wiffle ball or Nerf ball
- ✓ tape
- ✓ table

SKIN COLOR

As early forms of humans spread across the world, variations in skin color and body shape may have allowed some to adapt to local climates better than others. In Africa's warmth, dark skin was probably an advantage. In Europe and northern Asia's cold winters, light skin was likely advantageous. To see why, hold a sheet of white paper in one hand and a sheet of black paper in the other. Hold both sheets in front of a sunny window or a bright lightbulb. Through which sheet does more light pass?

In warm, sunny climates, dark skin reduced the likelihood of skin cancer because less light could penetrate the skin. In colder, northern climates with less sunlight, white skin allowed light to reach the cells where vitamin D is manufactured. Vitamin D is needed for strong bones.

BODY SHAPE, SURFACE AREA, AND RATE OF HEAT LOSS

Fossil evidence reveals that a member of the genus *Homo*—namely, *Homo neanderthalensis*, or Neanderthal Man—lived in Europe from 300,000 to 30,000 years ago. The fossilized skeletons of Neanderthals indicate that they were relatively short (163 cm [64 inches] in average height) and stocky. Such a body would be an adaptation for life in a cold climate. To see why, mold a piece of clay into a cube that is 5 cm on a side. Measure the surface area of the cube. You will see that its surface area is 150 square centimeters, because

$$\text{area of each side} = 5 \text{ cm} \times 5 \text{ cm} = 25 \text{ cm}^2$$
$$\text{There are 6 sides, so } 6 \times 25 \text{ cm}^2 = 150 \text{ cm}^2$$

Let the cube serve as a model of a typical short, stocky Neanderthal. Next, modify the same volume of clay to serve as a model of an average early human in Africa, where the climate was warmer. Fossil evidence from Africa indicates these hominids, who lived at about the same time as Neanderthals, were taller and slimmer. To take that fact into account, modify the clay so that its base is 4 cm × 4 cm. Its height will then be about 7.8 cm. What is the total surface area of this clay model?

Based on these two models, do you see why Neanderthals were more adapted to a cold climate than early humans in Africa?

If you don't, try this experiment. You will need a large jar, a teacup and a saucer. Fill the jar with hot tap water. Use a thermometer to find the temperature of the water and record it. Then fill the teacup about three-fourths full using water from the large jar. Pour the water in the teacup into the saucer. Fill the teacup to the same level again with the hot water from the jar. Place the teacup next to the saucer. After fifteen minutes, measure the temperature of the water in the teacup and in the saucer. Did the water in the teacup or the water in the saucer lose more heat during the fifteen-minute period? How can you tell? Did the water in the cup or in the saucer have more surface exposed to the cooler air? What does this experiment reveal about the effect of surface area on the rate at which heat is lost from a warm body? How might body shape have been an adaptation to climate for early humans living in Africa and Neanderthals living in Europe?

BINOCULAR VISION

One adaptation we share with all other primates (and many other predators) is the location of our eyes. Many animals have their eyes on opposite sides of their heads. Primates have both eyes on the front of their heads. This allows primates to see the same object with both eyes, which is called binocular vision.

To see the advantage of binocular vision, ask a friend to hold a pencil in front of you about waist high. Cover one eye and try to touch the tip of the pencil your friend is holding with the tip of a pencil that you hold. Repeat the experiment with the other eye closed. Finally, do the experiment using both eyes. Were you more accurate using two eyes or one?

Use a pencil to make a dot near the center of a sheet of paper. With one eye closed, try to quickly touch the dot with the tip of the pencil. Try it several times. Then do it again with both eyes open. Was it easier to do with one eye or with two?

Have a friend throw you a Wiffle or a Nerf ball. With one eye closed, use one hand to try to catch the ball twenty times. Then try it with the other eye closed. Finally, try it with both eyes open. In which case did you succeed in catching the ball more times?

Most primates, particularly the species that have been on

Earth the longest, live in trees. They often jump from one tree limb to another as they travel through a forest or jungle. How has binocular vision helped the survival of these primates?

OPPOSABLE THUMB

Humans, like all primates, have hands with strong flexible fingers, an adaptation for grasping tree limbs. Notice that you can touch every finger with your thumb. This makes it possible to carry out very delicate manipulations. It allows you to use tools. Scientists have discovered that primates, particularly chimpanzees and gorillas, also use simple tools such as sticks.

Your hands have many uses. You can use them as hooks to carry suitcases or pails; as power tools to squeeze an orange or make a meatball; or as a precision tool to thread a needle or write a sentence. You can also use your hands or fists as hammers, scoops, and signaling devices. Make a list of all the ways you use your hands, thumbs, and fingers. You will then realize how useful, flexible, and adaptable they are.

Another way to appreciate the importance of your thumb as an adaptation for survival by natural selection is to have someone tape your thumbs to the side of your palms. Then try to do some of the things you do every day—throw a ball, make a phone call, write a list of things to do, pick up a book, tie your shoes, eat a meal, and so on. How long does it take before you want the tape removed?

A BIPEDAL GAIT AND A BIG BRAIN

The two most important human adaptations are brain size and the ability to walk upright on two feet. The big toes of other primates are thumblike and, with the other toes, can be used to grasp objects. Human feet have adapted for walking upright. The big toe is in line with the other toes, making it easy to stride and run.

Make a list of the advantages humans have because they are able to walk upright. Make a second list of the many advantages that come from having a brain more than three times the size of any other primate.

- ◆ Prepare cubes of different dimensions. What happens to the ratio of surface area to volume as the cubes increase in size? What effect does doubling the sides of a cube have on the ratio of its surface area to its volume?

- ◆ Design a way to find the volume and surface area of human bodies. Can you predict the relative surface-area-to-volume ratios of different people just by looking at them?

- ◆ Make ice shapes that all have the same volume. You might prepare a cube and a sphere, as well as rectangular solids and cylinders of various dimensions. How can you predict which shape will melt fastest? Slowest?

BIG BRAIN OR WALKING UPRIGHT: WHICH CAME FIRST?

Darwin and many anthropologists believed human ancestors developed a large brain before they began to walk on two feet, or that the two adaptations evolved together. Recent fossil evidence shows they were wrong.

In 1974, a team of paleoanthropologists led by Donald Johanson uncovered 47 bones of an early hominid skeleton that came to be known as Lucy. Her official species name is *Australopithecus afarensis* for the Afar region of Ethiopia where she was found. The age of her bones, determined by radioactive dating of the rocky terrain where her fossil lay, showed that she lived about 3.2 million years ago.

Lucy was only 1.06 m (3 ft, 6 in) tall, about the size of a human six-year-old. Her brain size was that of a chimpanzee, but her legs and pelvis indicated that she walked erect. Lucy provided solid evidence that our early ancestors had walked erect before they acquired larger brains.

Because they walked upright, the *Australopithecus afarensis* species possessed hands that were free to carry food, hold babies, pick berries, throw stones, and make and use simple tools.

However, there is no evidence that *Australopithecus afarensis* used tools. It may have been another million years before another species, probably *Homo habilis*, actually made tools.

Lucy's pelvis, unlike the narrow pelvis of a chimpanzee, was bowl-shaped like a human's. The birth canal, however, was kidney-shaped rather than circular like a human's. Her femur (upper legbone) was very similar to a human's. The same was true of her knee and the rest of her lower body. Additional discoveries of *Australopithecus afarensis* fossils confirmed the fact that this species walked erect. However, their short legs and long arms gave them an apelike appearance. They had curved hands, typical of limb-grasping primates, suggesting they may have spent some of their time in trees. Perhaps they slept in trees to avoid predators.

Lucy's erect posture was confirmed in 1978 when a team led by Mary Leakey found ancient footprints embedded in volcanic ash near Laetoli, Tanzania. Radioactive dating of the ash indicated the footprints, made by two individuals apparently walking side by side, were made 3.6 million years ago.

The tracks, made by humanlike feet, probably belonged to the same species as Lucy. They were made by feet with big toes in line with the others, not turned outward like an ape's. The 69 tracks made a 23-meter (76-ft) trail along a straight path in damp volcanic ash. The footprints of the larger individual, perhaps a male, were 21.5 cm (8.5 in) long and about 47.2 cm

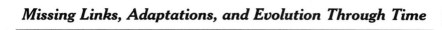

(18.6 in) apart. The others were 18.5 cm (7.3 in) long and 38.6 cm (15.2 in) apart. If we assume a ratio of 0.15 to 1 for foot to height, these two individuals were 1.4 m (4 ft, 7 in) and 1.2 m (3 ft, 11 in) tall. If the males of this species were taller than the females, the tracks may have been made by a male and a female a little taller than Lucy.

Chapter 4

Mendel, Genetics, and the Missing Key to Evolution

Darwin's theory of evolution depended on there being variations among members of a species. However, Darwin was never able to explain why variations occur. His critics attacked him on this weak point in his theory. At that time, people believed inherited traits blend, that offspring are a melding of their parents' traits. Consequently, critics argued, any variation providing an advantage in the struggle for survival would soon disappear. The variation would be diluted when it blended with the traits of the variant's mate. Their offspring's traits would be further blended by mating with average individuals.

Gregor Mendel (1822–1884), an Austrian monk, did experiments to find out how living things come to differ. His work is the foundation of genetics. He discovered why variations in a species persist. Characteristics do not blend; a characteristic, including a variation, can be transmitted through many generations.

Mendel began growing pea plants in his monastery's garden in 1856, three years before Darwin published *On the Origin of Species*. However, Mendel's work went unnoticed until it was rediscovered by Hugo de Vries in 1900. Early in the twentieth century, scientists realized that genes, located on chromosomes, control the development and traits of an organism. But the chemistry of genes and the way they function was not discovered until the second half of the century—only a few dozen years ago.

GREGOR MENDEL, THE FATHER OF GENETICS: HIS INITIAL EXPERIMENTS

Mendel investigated seven traits in pea plants. These traits were height, seed shape, color of the first leaves to sprout (cotyledons), seed coats, pod shape, pod color, and position of pods on the stem (see Figure 16).

Mendel started with true-breeding varieties—plants that for many generations showed only one of the two forms for any of the seven traits he studied. He crossed (mated) true-breeding plants that had contrasting traits. (These plants were known as the parent or P_1 generation.) To make these crosses, he

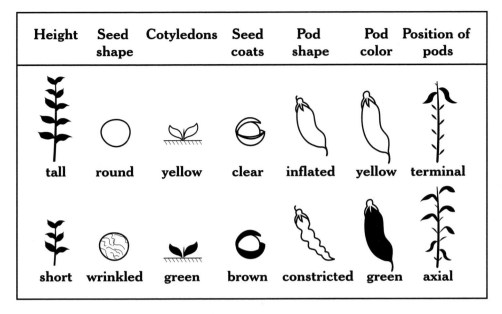

Height	Seed shape	Cotyledons	Seed coats	Pod shape	Pod color	Position of pods
tall	round	yellow	clear	inflated	yellow	terminal
short	wrinkled	green	brown	constricted	green	axial

Figure 16.

These are the seven traits that vary in the pea plants investigated by Gregor Mendel.

removed the stamens from, say, the flowers of a tall plant and placed their pollen on the pistils of a short plant. He also removed the stamens from the flowers of short plants and placed their pollen grains on the pistils of tall plants. This prevented the plants from self-pollinating, which is normally the way pea plants reproduce. He then covered the flowers to prevent pollination by wind or insects.

The seeds produced by the flowers from the P_1 generation were planted and observed. The plants that grew from these seeds, known as the first filial or F_1 generation, flowered and were allowed to self-pollinate. The seeds produced by the F_1 generation grew into the plants of the second filial or F_2 generation.

MENDEL'S RESULTS

When true-breeding tall plants were crossed with true-breeding short plants in the P_1 generation, all the F_1 plants that grew from their seeds were tall. There were no short plants. So much for the blending theory of inheritance! However, the factor for shortness had not disappeared. When the F_1 plants self-pollinated to produce the F_2 generation, the results were striking. Both tall and short plants grew from these seeds. The factor for shortness, hidden in the F_1 generation, reappeared in one-fourth of the F_2 plants. The other three-fourths were tall. The ratio of tall to short was 3:1.

When the F_2 generation plants reproduced by self-pollination, Mendel found that all the short plants were true-breeding. They produced only short offspring. One third of the tall plants were true-breeding; they produced only tall offspring. The other two-thirds produced both tall and short plants in the same ratio (3:1) as their F_1 ancestors. Table 3 summarizes Mendel's results.

Mendel found similar results when he crossed plants for each of the other six contrasting traits. His results for the F_1 and F_2 generations for each of the seven traits he studied are shown in Table 4. In all cases, the F_2 plants produced the same 3:1 pattern of offspring.

Table 3:

MENDEL'S RESULTS FROM PEA PLANT CROSSING.

Generation	Cross	Offspring from seeds
P_1	tall × short? $\rightarrow$	F_1: all tall
F_1	tall × tall? $\rightarrow$	F_2: 3 tall: 1 short
F_2	short × short? $\rightarrow$	F_3: all short
	1/3 tall × tall? $\rightarrow$	F_3: all tall
	2/3 tall × tall? $\rightarrow$	F_3: 3 tall: 1 short

This table shows Mendel's results when he crossed true-breeding tall pea plants with true-breeding short pea plants (P_1 generation). An × is used to indicate a cross (mating) between plants.

The results show that in the F_2 generation, one trait is three times as likely to appear as the other. The trait that appears three times as frequently is the same one that appears in all plants in the F_1 generation. Mendel referred to the trait that appeared more frequently in the F_2 generation as a dominant trait. A trait that disappeared in the F_1 generation, such as shortness, he called a recessive trait. When both traits were present in a seed, only the dominant one was seen. Thus, in pea plants, tallness is a dominant trait, while shortness is a recessive trait. From Table 4, can you identify the dominant and recessive traits in each of the other six characteristics Mendel investigated?

Table 4:

INVESTIGATION OF SEVEN TRAITS FOR THE F_1 AND F_2 GENERATIONS OF PEA PLANTS.

P_1 cross	F_1 Plants	F_2 Plants	Ratio
tall × short	all were tall	787 were tall 277 were short	2.84:1
round × wrinkled seeds	all were round	5474 were round 1850 were wrinkled	2.96:1
yellow × green cotyledons	all were yellow	6022 were yellow 2001 were green	3.01:1
brown × clear seed coats	all were brown	705 were brown 224 were clear	3.15:1
inflated × constricted pods	all were inflated	882 were inflated 299 were constricted	2.95:1
green × yellow pods	all were green	428 were green 152 were yellow	2.82:1
axial × terminal pods	all were axial	651 were axial 207 were terminal	3.14:1

Mendel investigated seven traits inherited by pea plants. The results for the F_1 and F_2 generations for each trait are shown above.

Experiment 4.1

A Model to Explain Mendel's Initial Experiments

Materials

- ✓ 24 dry, dark-colored bean seeds similar in size and shape
- ✓ 2 paper cups
- ✓ 24 dry, light-colored bean seeds similar in size and shape
- ✓ notebook
- ✓ pencil

Without reading any further, see if you can develop a model (theory) to explain the results of Mendel's experiments.

Now compare your model with Mendel's. He assumed that hereditary factors are passed to the next generation through the parent plants' gametes (from the Greek *gamein*, "to marry"), which are the sperm cells in the pollen and the egg cells in the pistil.

Use the dark beans to represent the factor for tall pea plants. Use light-colored beans to represent the factor for short pea plants. Place two dozen dark beans in one paper cup. This cup represents the tall pea plant. Place an equal number of light-colored beans in a second cup. This cup represents the short pea plant.

Since inherited factors come from both parents, let's assume, as Mendel did, that in the P_1 generation the purebred tall plants have only the factor for tallness, represented by the dark beans. Purebred short plants have only the factor for shortness, represented by the light-colored beans. Let's assume also, as Mendel did, that the F_1 generation receives only one factor for height from each parent (see Figures 17a and 17b).

In your model this can be done by taking one bean from each of the two cups and putting them together. Another way is to make a Punnett square (devised by English geneticist Reginald Punnett, 1875–1967) and let letters represent the inherited factors. Figure 17c shows how to make a Punnett square for the P_1 and the F_1 crosses where tallness is involved. The symbols representing the inherited factors for one parent are listed along the side of the square. The symbols representing the inherited factors for the other parent are listed along the top. Each possible combination of inherited factors that can be found in the offspring are listed inside the square. By counting the number of times a combination appears in the square you can predict the likelihood of that trait appearing in the offspring.

As you can see from Figure 17a, Figure 17b, and the first Punnett square in Figure 17c, all the F_1 offspring will be tall. The factor for tallness, represented by the dark bean or the capital letter T, is dominant to the factor for shortness, represented by the light-colored bean or the small letter *t*. When the

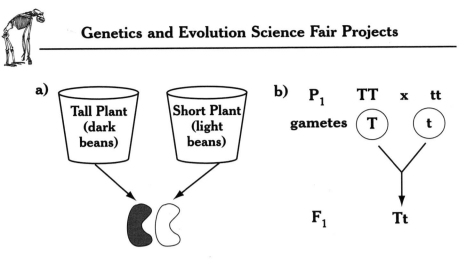

a)

| Tall Plant (dark beans) | Short Plant (light beans) |

b) P$_1$ TT   x   tt

gametes   T   t

F$_1$ Tt

c) Punnett square for P$_1$ generation TT x tt

	T	T
t	Tt	Tt
t	Tt	Tt

Punnett square for F$_1$ generation TT x tt

	T	t
T	TT	Tt
t	Tt	tt

Figure 17.

a) Pure-breeding tall plants have only the factor for tallness, represented here by dark beans. Pure-breeding short plants have only the factor for shortness, represented here by light-colored beans. The F$_1$ generation receives one factor for height from each parent. All F$_1$ plants will be tall, because tallness is the dominant factor. b) The cross between tall and short plants can also be represented by symbols—T for tallness and t for shortness. Gametes from the tall plants all carry the factor T. Gametes from the short plants all carry the factor t. Cells of the F$_1$ plants have both factors, T and t, but they are tall because T is dominant to t. c) The diagrams show Punnett squares for the P$_1$ and F$_1$ generations.

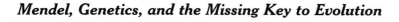

hereditary factors for both tall and short plants are present in a plant's cells, the plant will be tall.

What hereditary factors for height will be in the gametes produced by plants of the F_1 generation? What kind of offspring will be produced?

The second Punnett square shows that the inherited factors, T and t, can combine in three different ways: TT, Tt, and tt. Since T is dominant to t, three of every four F_1 offspring will be tall (TT, Tt, and Tt) and one (tt) will be short.

To see how this works in a more concrete way, place 12 dark beans and 12 light-colored beans in one cup. Cover the cup with your hand and shake it to thoroughly mix the beans. Do the same with a second paper cup. Each cup contains the hereditary factors for height that can be in a gamete produced by an F_1 pea plant. Each cup represents a parent plant from the F_1 generation. Each bean represents a hereditary factor that can be found in a sperm or egg cell (the gametes).

Close your eyes and remove a bean (representing a factor for height) from one cup. This bean is the hereditary factor that will be in the sperm. Then repeat the procedure for the other cup. This is the hereditary factor that will be in the egg. The two beans together represent the hereditary factors that will be in the seed.

Record the result in your notebook. If you drew two dark beans, record it as TT because the factors for height from both parents were for tallness. (The capital T shows that it is a dominant factor.) If you drew two light-colored beans, record it as tt. (The small letter t shows that it is a recessive factor, the factor for shortness.) If you drew a dark bean and a light-colored bean, record it as Tt. (This seed will produce a tall plant, but it also carries the factor for shortness.)

Return the beans to their respective cups. Shake the cups again. Repeat the process of drawing one bean from each cup and recording the result 100 times. Be sure to return the beans to their respective cups and shake them after each drawing. These paired factors illustrate the way factors would join to form 100 seeds of the next (F_2) generation. What would be the height of the plants produced by each of the seeds whose factors you recorded? How many will be tall? How many will be short? Based on your data, what percentage of the F_2 generation will be tall? What percentage will be short? Of those that are tall, what percentage will be true-breeding—have only the hereditary factors for tallness (two dark beans)? (Such plants are said to be *homozygous* [from the Greek words *homo*, "same," and *zygou*, "yoked"] because both factors are the same.) Notice that all the short plants are homozygous. What percentage will have a factor for both tall and short (Tt: one dark bean and one light-colored bean)? Such plants are said to be *heterozygous* (from the Greek *hetero*, "different").

How do the percentages of tall and short plants in the F_2 generation that you obtained in your experiment compare with Mendel's results (see Table 4)? Why might your percentages be different from his?

The Role of Probability in Heredity

Materials

✓ 2 pennies, one bright
and shiny and one
tarnished and dull

✓ a partner
✓ pencil
✓ notebook

To see how *expected results* may be modified by probability, use two pennies, one bright and one tarnished and dull, to represent gametes from two members of the heterozygous F_1 generation (Tt). The head side of the bright penny represents the dominant factor for tallness (T_1), its tail side represents the factor for shortness (t_1). Similarly, the head side of the dull penny represents the tallness factor from a second plant (T_2); the tail side represents the factor for shortness (t_2).

Each coin has the same chance of turning up heads as it does tails. Consequently, if the two coins are tossed at the same time, the probability of two heads can be expected in one-fourth of the trials. The same is true of two tails. That means a head matched with a tail can be expected in one-half the trials. Figure 18 shows why such outcomes can be expected.

Ask a friend to flip one of the pennies, while you flip the other at the same time. Let the pennies fall to the floor. Then record the results in a data table like the one in Table 5. Use

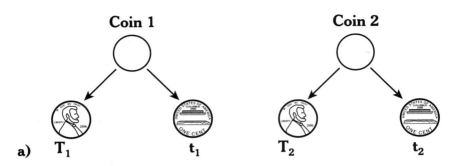

Figure 18.

a) Two pennies are tossed. Each has an equal probability of landing heads or tails. b) One way to show the probabilities is to list the possibilities for one penny along a horizontal axis and the possibilities for the other penny along a vertical axis. As you can see, both coins can be expected to land heads up in one-fourth of the trials. The same is true for their both landing tails up. One heads and one tails can be expected in half the trials.

simple check marks like the ones shown in Table 5 to record the result of each toss of the coins.

After 12 tosses, what would you expect the results to be? How many times would you expect both coins to be heads? Both tails? One heads and one tails?

What are the actual results? How do they compare with your prediction?

Table 5:

A DATA TABLE FOR RECORDING THE RESULTS OF TOSSING TWO COINS AT THE SAME TIME.

Both heads(T_1T_2)	Both tails(t_1t_2)	Bright heads/Dull tails(T_1t_2)	Dull heads/Bright tails(T_2t_1)
✓	✓	✓	✓

The results of four hypothetical tosses are shown. The results of your first four tosses may be different.

What are the results after 50 tosses of the two coins? After 100 tosses? After 200 tosses? How does the number of tosses affect the actual results as compared to the expected results? Why do you think Mendel used hundreds of plants in his experiments? Why was Mendel's knowledge of mathematics useful to him in doing his experiments?

Science Project Idea

Three coins are tossed at the same time. What is the probability that all three coins will be heads? That all three coins will be tails? What are the other possibilities? What is the probability of each possibility? Try to confirm your predictions by experiment.

ANOTHER OF MENDEL'S EXPERIMENTS

Mendel had crossed plants homozygous for green pods with plants homozygous for yellow pods. His results revealed that all members of the F_1 generation had green pods. Which trait is dominant?

When members of the F_1 generation were crossed, the F_2 generation showed a ratio of 3 plants with green pods for every 1 plant with yellow pods. Make a Punnett square to show the results of crossing purebred plants that had yellow pods with purebred plants that had green pods. Make another Punnett square to show the F_1 cross.

Mendel wondered what would happen if he examined two pairs of hereditary factors through several generations of pea plants. Would they behave as separate factors or would they stick together?

To find out, he crossed true-breeding tall plants that had green pods with true-breeding short plants that had yellow pods. He found that all the plants in the F_1 generation were tall and bore green pods. The results did not surprise him because tallness and green pods were both dominant traits.

When he crossed plants from the F_1 generation, he found that $9/16$ of the F_2 plants were tall and had green pods, $3/16$ were tall with yellow pods, $3/16$ were short with green pods, and $1/16$ had both recessive traits. They were short and had yellow pods. This was a ratio of 9:3:3:1.

Modeling the Inheritance of Two Independent Traits

Materials

✓ 48 dry dark beans

✓ 48 dry light-colored beans of the same size and shape

✓ 48 dry green split peas

✓ 48 dry yellow split peas

✓ 4 paper cups

✓ pencil

✓ notebook

Mendel was not surprised by the results of his experiment. Were you? See if you can develop a model to explain the 9:3:3:1 ratio he obtained in the F_2 generation. Remember, in his P_1 generation, plants homozygous for tallness and green pods were crossed with plants homozygous for shortness and yellow pods.

Now compare your model with Mendel's. Mendel assumed that hereditary factors are independent of one another and are passed independently to the next generation through the plant's gametes. To see how this works, once again represent the factor for tall plants with dark beans and the factor for short plants with light-colored beans. Dry green split peas can be used to represent the dominant factor for green pods. Dry yellow split peas can be used to represent the recessive factor for yellow pods.

T represents the factor for tallness, t the factor for shortness. Let G represent the dominant factor for green pods and g the recessive factor for yellow pods. From Experiment 4.1, you know that the F_1 generation will be heterozygous for both height (Tt) and pod color (Gg). Figure 19 shows the gametes produced by the P_1 plants and the factors found in the F_1 generation.

Now make a model of the factors for height and pod color in the F_1 plants. Place two dozen dark beans and an equal number of light-colored beans in the same paper cup (cup 1). Do the same with a second cup (cup 2).

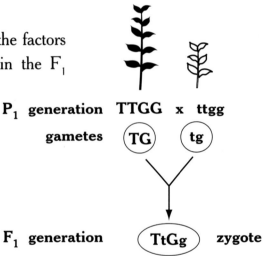

Figure 19.

These diagrams show a cross between plants homozygous for tallness (TT) and green pods (GG) with plants homozygous for shortness (tt) and yellow pods (gg). Gametes from one group of plants carry the factors T and G. Gametes from the other group of plants carry the factors t and g. The F_1 generation plants will all be tall with green pods. However, they will be heterozygous for these traits (TtGg). What types of gametes will the F_1 generation produce (TtGg × TtGg)?

Cover each cup with your hand and shake it to thoroughly mix the seeds. The two kinds of beans represent the hereditary factors for height that can be in a gamete from an F_1 pea plant. The reason for the two cups is that one factor for height comes from each of two parents.

Add two dozen dry green split peas and an equal number of dry yellow split peas to a third paper cup (cup 3). Do the same with a fourth cup (cup 4). Cover each cup with your hand and shake it to thoroughly mix the seeds.

Put cup 1 with beans and cup 3 with split peas next to one another. Place cups 2 and 4 close to one another but apart from the first two. Pair 1 and 3 and pair 2 and 4 contain the factors for height and pod color present in a parent. The "gametes" from these two parents will be joined to form the seeds of the F_2 generation. Each gamete will contain a hereditary factor for height and pod color.

Close your eyes and reach into a cup 1. Remove one bean from the cup. Do the same for cup 3. Put these two "hereditary factors" together. They represent the factors for height and pod color that will be in a gamete from one parent. Similarly, join the hereditary factors for height and pod color that will be in a gamete from the second parent (cups 2 and 4). Mendel assumed, as you have, that each seed receives one factor for height and one factor for pod color from each parent as shown by the Punnett square in Figure 20.

F₁ male		**Possible sperm cells**	
TtGg ⟶	(TG) (Tg) (tG) (tg)		

F₁ male → TtGg → Possible sperm cells (TG) (Tg) (tG) (tg)

F₁ female → TtGg → Possible egg cells (TG) (Tg) (tG) (tg)

Punnett square to show all possible combinations of gametes in the F₂ generation

	TG	Tg	tG	tg
TG	TTGG	TTGg	TtGG	TtGg
Tg	TTGg	TTgg	TtGg	Ttgg
tG	TtGG	TtGg	ttGG	ttGg
tg	TtGg	Ttgg	ttGg	ttgg

Figure 20.

The F₁ generation is heterozygous for height and pod color (TtGg). They can produce four types of gametes for these two traits. The Punnett square shows the gametes and the factors in the 16 possible types of seeds that can form when gametes from the parents unite. What fraction of the F₂ plants can be expected to be tall with green pods? Tall with yellow pods? Short with green pods? Short with yellow pods?

Any organism has both a *phenotype* and a *genotype*. Its phenotype is its appearance, the way it looks. Its genotype is its genetic makeup, the genes it contains. For example, suppose you have a pea plant that inherited factors for tallness and yellow pods from one parent (Tg) and factors for shortness and green pods from the other (tG). The plant's phenotype is tall with

green pods. Its genotype with respect to height and pod color is TtGg (heterozygous tall and heterozygous for green pods).

Record the phenotype and genotype of the plant that will be produced by the "gametes" you have just joined.

Put the beans and peas back in the cups from which they came. Cover the cups and shake them to mix the seeds. Repeat the process 99 more times so that you will have the results of 100 different unions of gametes. Record phenotype and genotype for each trial.

Examine your results. Will any of the seeds produce plants that are short with yellow pods? If so, what fraction of the 100 plants have both these recessive traits? What fraction will be tall and have green pods? What fraction will be tall and have yellow pods? What fraction will be short and have green pods?

How closely do your results agree with the 9:3:3:1 phenotype ratio that Mendel expected from the cross TtGg x TtGg?

Science Project Idea

Develop a model to explain the various offspring that can be expected in the F_1 and F_2 generations from a P_1 cross of plants homozygous for tallness, round seeds, and green pods with plants that are short with wrinkled seeds and yellow pods.

Chapter 5

Mendel, Genes, Chromosomes, and Models

H ugo de Vries (1848–1935) was studying the inherited traits of primroses when he rediscovered Mendel's experiments while searching the literature for experiments similar to his own. De Vries realized that he and Mendel had reached the same conclusions.

But de Vries had observed that every once in a while a new variety of primrose would suddenly appear. He had discovered what Darwin had sought—an underlying cause of evolution.

The sudden appearance of a new trait was called a mutation (from a Latin word, *mutare*, meaning "to change"). Experiments showed that mutations could be passed to offspring. If the change provided an adaptation that enabled them to better cope with their environment, then they were more likely to survive than other members of the species. Over time, the accumulation of mutations could lead to a new species.

Mendel discovered how traits are transmitted from generation to generation. De Vries discovered that mutations are also transmitted, the explanation for variation within a species. Had the experiments of Mendel and de Vries preceded Darwin's work, far less controversy would have followed Darwin's book *On the Origin of Species.*

Mutations are significant in medicine and insect control. Disease-causing bacteria targeted by an antibiotic can suddenly become resistant. A mutation can create a new strain resistant to the antibiotic. While most insects are killed by insecticide, a few mutants will have a gene that allows them to tolerate the chemical. In a short time, this strain of insect becomes the predominant form. The insecticide is no longer effective. A new insecticide is developed to kill the mutant form, and guess what! Another mutation leads to insects that are resistant to the new insecticide.

CHROMOSOMES AND GENES

As microscopes improved, details inside plant and animal cells were observed. Most cells contained a spherical object called the nucleus. Surrounding the nucleus was the jellylike cytoplasm. Although the types of cytoplasm in muscle, nerve, connective, blood, and epithelial cells were quite different, their nuclei were similar.

In 1879, Walther Flemming (1843–1905), a German anatomist, found that material within the nuclei of cells absorbed a red dye he was using to stain cells. He called this stringlike material chromatin, from the Greek word for color (*chrōma*). He noticed that as a cell began to divide, the chromatin became shorter and thicker, forming what came to be known as chromosomes ("colored bodies"). Flemming was able to observe chromosomes at different stages of cell division, a process he called mitosis.

During mitosis, the membrane surrounding the nucleus breaks down and thin fibers (spindle fibers) form and attach to the chromosomes. Each chromosome replicates itself so that the number of chromosomes doubles. The duplicates separate and are pulled to opposite sides of the cell as two new cells form. Each new cell has the same number of chromosomes as the parent cell.

Biologists who studied mitosis were puzzled. If gametes have the same number of chromosomes as other cells, then a zygote (formed by the union of sperm and egg cells) would have twice as many chromosomes as the parents. Since all the cells of an organism come from repeated mitotic division of the zygote, the number of chromosomes in the cells would double in each successive generation.

Careful observations of cell division leading to gametes provided an answer. Unlike other cells, gametes are formed by a different type of cell division known as meiosis, from a Greek word meaning "to diminish." During meiosis, only one member of each pair of chromosomes reaches a sperm or egg cell. Consequently, the number of chromosomes in gametes is half the number found in other cells. When gametes unite to form a zygote, the chromosomes pair off again and the number of chromosomes per cell is restored to the number typical of the species. For humans, that number is 46 (23 pairs).

Chromosomes provide the means for transmitting inherited traits from parents to offspring. They are believed to be made up of smaller chemical units, called genes—the source of inherited traits. The factors for the yellow or green color of peas, the height of the pea plants, the color of human eyes, and all other inherited characteristics are transmitted by genes found along the chromosomes of gametes.

Experiment 5.1

A Model of Mitosis

Materials

✓ 12 white pipe cleaners or twist ties

✓ colored felt-tip pen

✓ sheet of paper

To help you understand what happens to chromosomes during mitosis, you can use pipe cleaners or twist ties to represent chromosomes. On a sheet of paper, draw a large circle to represent a cell. Draw a vertical line (the equator) down the center of the circle. Prepare four (two pairs of) "chromosomes" as shown in Figure 21a. Bend one pair. Color one member of each pair with a felt-tip pen so you can distinguish it from its twin. These are the chromosomes found in this hypothetical cell.

Line up the "chromosomes," one after the other, close to the center line of the cell you drew on paper (see Figure 21b). Because the chromosomes replicated at an earlier stage of mitosis, you should prepare four more chromosomes identical to the first four. Place them next to their identical partners, as shown in Figure 21c. Next, separate the identical chromosomes as occurs during a later stage of mitosis (Figure 21d). Finally (Figure 21e), draw a wide line between the separated chromosomes to show that cell division has occurred.

How does the number of chromosomes in the two new cells compare with the number that was in the original cell? How does the number of pairs of chromosomes in the two new cells compare with the number of pairs were in the original nucleus?

If these pipe cleaners or twist ties represent the number of chromosomes characteristic of a particular species, how many pairs of chromosomes are in each body cell of a member of this species? How many chromosomes will be found in the gametes

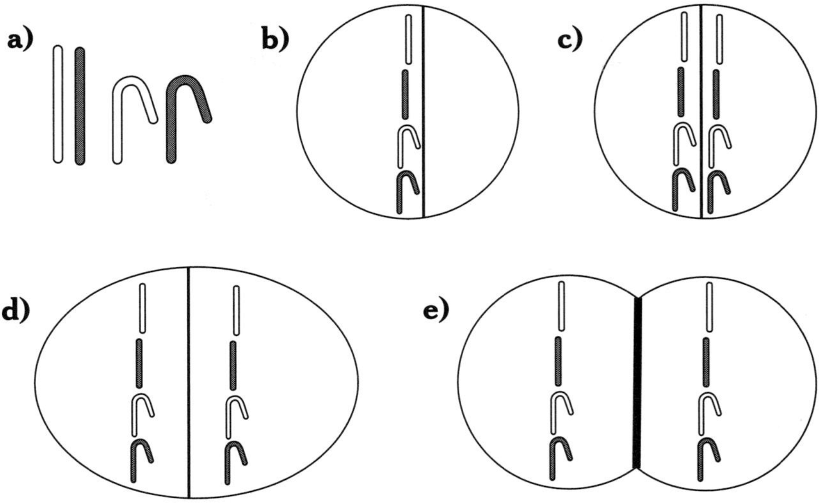

Figure 21.

Pipe cleaners or twist ties can be used to model chromosomes in cells undergoing mitosis (division of body cells).

produced by this species? How many members of each pair of chromosomes will be in the gametes of this species?

Experiment 5.2

A Model of Meiosis

Materials

✓ pieces of colored yarn, preferably green, yellow, and dark

✓ pipe cleaners or twist ties
✓ sheets of paper
✓ pencil

A physical model is even more helpful in understanding what happens to chromosomes during meiosis when sperm or egg cells are produced. You will need twice as many pipe cleaners or twist ties as you did in Experiment 5.1. Prepare four (two pairs of) model chromosomes. Do this twice so that you have a total of 8 chromosomes, as shown in Figure 22a.

Attach a small piece of green yarn to one member of each pair of the straight chromosomes. The yarn will represent the gene for green pod color. To the mate in each pair, at a corresponding place, attach a small piece of yellow yarn to represent the gene for yellow pod color.

To one member of each pair of the hook-shaped chromosomes, attach a long piece of dark yarn to represent the gene for tallness. To its mate in each pair, at a corresponding place, attach a short piece of dark yarn to represent the gene for shortness.

These are the "genes" and "chromosomes" that would be present in the F_1 generation following a cross of pea plants homozygous for green pods and tallness with short plants that produce yellow pods.

On a sheet of paper, draw two large circles to represent two cells. Draw a vertical line (the equator) down the center of each. Line up the chromosomes in pairs along the equator of each cell to represent the beginning of meiosis. (During meiosis, the chromosomes line up in pairs.) As you can see from Figures 22b and 22b′, the two pairs of chromosomes can line up in two different ways. The straight chromosome with the gene for green

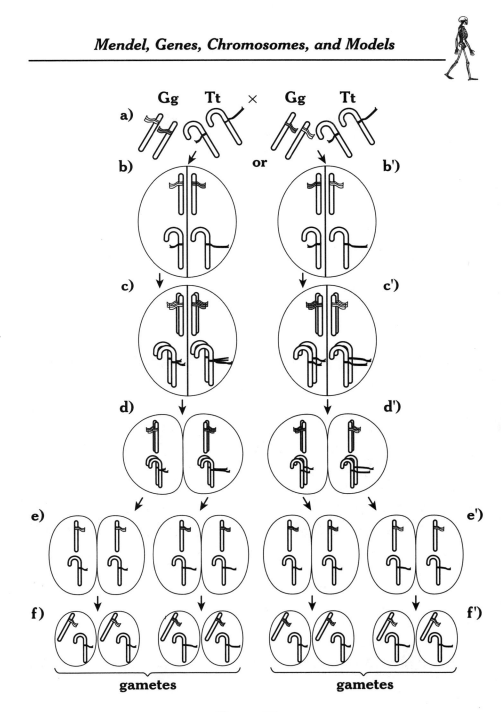

Figure 22.

During meiosis, only one member of each pair of chromosomes enters each gamete. This is accomplished by two cell divisions. Chromosomes replicate only before the first cell division.

pods can be on the same side of the equator as the hook-shaped chromosome carrying the gene for tallness, or on the same side as the one that carries the gene for shortness.

The chromosomes replicated at an earlier stage, forming four-chromosome clusters (known as tetrads). So use pipe cleaners or twist ties and colored yarn to prepare eight more chromosomes identical to the first eight. Place them next to their identical partners, as shown in Figures 22c and 22c′. Next, separate the identical chromosomes as happens during the first meiotic cell division (Figures 22d and 22d′). Draw a wide line between the separated chromosomes to show that the cell has divided.

If cell division stopped here, how many chromosomes would be in the gametes (sperm or egg cells)? How many chromosomes would be in the zygote formed by the union of sperm and egg cells? What would happen to the number of chromosomes in the cells of the organism in each succeeding generation?

The second cell division in meiosis reduces the chromosome number to half the number found in the other cells of the organism. To see how this happens, separate the chromosome pairs you have in each cell after the first cell division (Figures 22d and 22d′). Move them to opposite sides of a "cell" and draw a line to represent cell division, as shown in Figures 22e and 22e′. This represents the second meiotic division. Finally, place the chromosomes in cells that have separated into four distinct "gametes," as shown in Figures 22f and 22f′.

How does the number of chromosomes in the gametes compare with the number that were in the original parent cell prior to meiosis? How many members of each pair of chromosomes are in each gamete? How many distinct types of gametes are there? How many would there be in a species that has 4 pairs of chromosomes? Humans have 23 pairs of chromosomes. How many chromosomes would you expect to find in human egg or sperm cells?

Science Project Ideas

◆ Investigate how you might use an anther from a lily flower to prepare a slide that would reveal various stages of cells undergoing meiosis. Then examine these slides under a microscope.

◆ Use chromosome models to show that the traits Mendel studied must have been located on different chromosomes.

◆ Geneticists often use fruit flies, *Drosophila melanogaster*, in their work. The entire life cycle of fruit flies takes only 10 to 14 days, so several generations can be observed in a month's time. You might like to use them in some experiments. Through your school, you can buy *D. melanogaster* and the supplies needed to grow and experiment with them from almost any science supply house that sells biological materials (see Appendix). You might start by mating winged with wingless flies and then mate members of the F_1 generation.

GENES, A MOLD, AND SCIENCE

During the early 1940s, George W. Beadle and Edward L. Tatum carried out a series of experiments using a simple mold—*Neurospora crassa*. Their experimental results shed the first light on how genes work. Beadle and Tatum found that ordinary *N. crassa* spores (the reproductive units of mold) could grow on a simple medium that contained only sugar, salts, and biotin (a vitamin). From these simple chemicals, the mold could manufacture all the substances it needed to live.

The scientists X-rayed the mold and then placed its spores on the medium. Many of these spores did not grow on the medium. Beadle and Tatum hypothesized that the spores that did not grow had undergone a mutation that prevented them from making some essential protein or vitamin.

There are 20 amino acids essential in making the proteins found in living cells. Beadle and Tatum used that knowledge to test their hypothesis. They placed X-rayed mold spores on a medium that contained all the 20 essential amino acids. In this complete medium, most of the spores grew.

To find which amino acid a mutant spore needed, they added various supplements to the simple medium until they found the one that allowed the mutant spores to grow.

The X-rayed spores could not produce a certain amino acid because they lacked an enzyme, a substance that helps a cell to work. The cells depended on the amino acid added to the simple medium. The manufacture of each enzyme was controlled by a specific gene. If that gene changed (mutated), the mold could not make the enzyme. Without the enzyme, the mold was unable to make an amino acid essential for life. The notion that each gene is associated with the manufacture of a specific enzyme became widely accepted.

GENES, DNA, AND THE ELECTRON MICROSCOPE

Scientists became certain that all genes, like the ones that controlled mold enzymes, were located on chromosomes. Chemists had found that chromosomes contained proteins and a substance called DNA (deoxyribonucleic acid).

With improvements to the electron microscope in the 1950s, it became possible to magnify objects a million times, a thousand times more than with ordinary microscopes. With such magnification, biologists at last were able to see the details of cell structure.

WATSON, CRICK, AND DNA

In 1953, James Watson and Francis Crick published their molecular model of DNA and the means by which it replicates (makes a copy of itself). The model of DNA they developed (see Figure 23) was a long, two-stranded, curved "ladder," known as a double helix; that is, a double spiral. The DNA molecule contained four different kinds of nucleotides, the basic units of the nucleic acid. Each nucleotide consists of a sugar (deoxyribose), a phosphate group, and a nitrogen-containing base. The sides of the ladder are the sugar and phosphate portions of the molecules, which are joined in a long chain. The sides of the ladder are connected by four bases that constitute the ladder's "rungs." The four bases are thymine, guanine, adenine, and cytosine.

Chemists who had analyzed DNA found that the number of molecules of adenine (A) and thymine (T) in DNA were always equal. They found, too, that the number of cytosine (C) and guanine (G) molecules were equal but not equal to the number of thymine or adenine molecules. Watson and Crick concluded that in DNA's long, double-helix-shaped molecule, the C and G bases were always bonded to one another. Similarly, the A and T bases were bonded to one another. If a vertical portion of one strand of the molecule has the bases ACTG, the corresponding adjacent portion of the strand will have the bases TGAC.

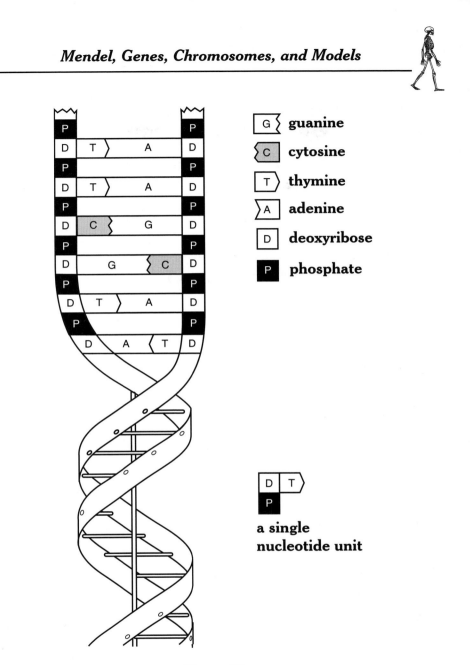

Figure 23.

Watson and Crick's model of DNA was a double helix similar to a spiral staircase. Two strands of deoxyribose sugar and phosphate groups constitute the sides. The rungs are made up of pairs of nitrogen-containing bases. Adenine is always paired with thymine, and guanine always joins with cytosine.

The bonds between the bases A and T or C and G that hold the strands of the double helix together are relatively weak. As a result, at the time of cell division, the strands can separate. Each strand then combines with nucleotides in the cytoplasm to create a duplicate of the strand from which it separated (Figure 24). The result is two identical double-helix molecules. Each molecule has a new strand and an old strand. The DNA has replicated, just as chromosomes replicate. In fact, as you might suspect, a chromosome consists of DNA wound around a protein framework.

FROM DNA TO GENES

Watson and Crick's model explained the structure of DNA and how it replicated during cell division. But where are the genes?

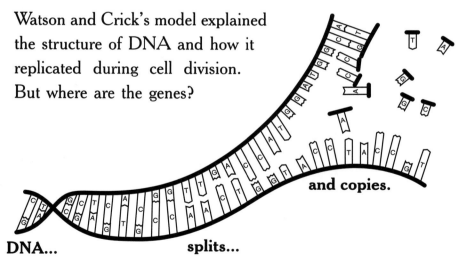

and copies.

DNA...   splits...

Figure 24.

During cell division, the DNA strand unzips and replicates by adding nucleotides to build new strands on each side of the old one.

And how do genes control the production of proteins, including the enzymes that govern the chemical reactions within cells? What code do they use?

Proteins are long chains of different amino acids joined together. The four bases (C, G, T, and A) alone can't be the code for joining amino acids, because there are 20 different essential amino acids and only 4 bases. Even combinations of two bases can't provide the code, because four bases, taken two at a time, can combine in only 16 different ways (see Table 6). However, four bases combined three at a time would provide 64 different combinations, more than enough to code for the 20 different amino acids.

Table 6:

THE SIXTEEN WAYS THAT FOUR BASES, TAKEN TWO AT A TIME, CAN COMBINE.

	A	T	C	G
A	AA	AT	AC	AG
T	TA	TT	TC	TG
C	CA	CT	CC	CG
G	GA	GT	GC	GG

Using electron microscopes, scientists found that proteins are made on tiny structures called ribosomes that lie in the cytoplasm outside the nucleus. But DNA is inside a cell's nucleus.

How could genes found in nuclear DNA code for proteins made in a cell's cytoplasm?

Experiments showed that RNA (ribonucleic acid), which is very similar to DNA, is found both inside and outside the nuclei of cells. RNA exists as single, rather than double, strands of nucleotides. RNA molecules are shorter than those of DNA, and they contain the base uracil (U) in place of thymine (T). During the formation of RNA, U, not T, bonds with A.

The code used in making proteins consists of groups of three bases, known as codons. The possible codons and the specific amino acids for which they code are shown in Figure 25. Since there are 64 possible codons and only 20 essential amino acids, there are more codons than there are essential amino acids. As a result, more than one codon may code for an amino acid. Some codons, such as UAA, UAG, and UGA, are used to signal an end to a chain of amino acids. AUG is sometimes used to signal the start of a protein as well as the production of the amino acid methionine.

As shown in Figure 26a, a form of RNA known as messenger RNA (mRNA) is made on a segment of DNA. The segment is a gene that provides the code for making a particular protein. The mRNA carries the genetic code through the nuclear membrane to the ribosomes in the cytoplasm (Figure 26b). Another type of RNA, known as transfer RNA (tRNA), attaches to the complementary part of the mRNA.

First Letter	Second Letter				Third Letter
	U	C	A	G	
U	Phenylalanine Phenylalanine Leucine Leucine	Serine Serine Serine Serine	Tyrosine Tyrosine Stop Stop	Cysteine Cysteine Stop Tryptophan	U C A G
C	Leucine Leucine Leucine Leucine	Proline Proline Proline Proline	Histidine Histidine Glutamine Glutamine	Arginine Arginine Arginine Arginine	U C A G
A	Isoleucine Isoleucine Isoleucine Methionine*	Threonine Threonine Threonine Threonine	Asparagine Asparagine Lysine Lysine	Serine Serine Arginine Arginine	U C A G
G	Valine Valine Valine Valine	Alanine Alanine Alanine Alanine	Aspartic Acid Aspartic Acid Glutamic Acid Glutamic Acid	Glycine Glycine Glycine Glycine	U C A G

* Also frequently a code to indicate where a gene starts on the DNA strand.

Figure 25.

The triplet codes (codons) for the 20 essential amino acids are shown here. The codes are carried by mRNA from genes on the DNA to the ribosomes in the cytoplasm. (U = uracil; C = cytosine; A = adenine; G = guanine.) For example, the table shows that the code for tryptophan is UGG and that one code for leucine is UUA. What are the other codes for leucine? What is signaled by UAG?

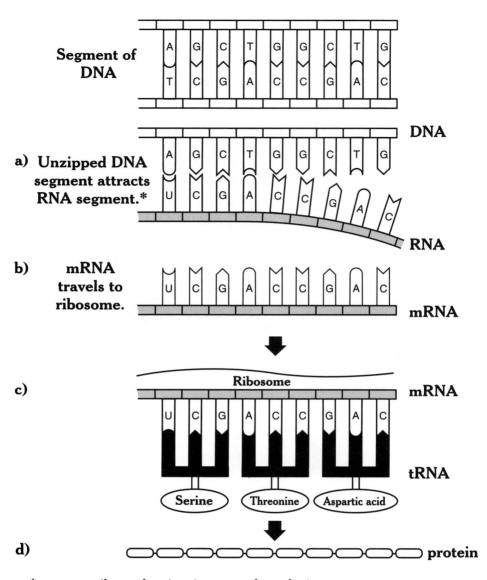

Segment of DNA

a) Unzipped DNA segment attracts RNA segment.*

b) mRNA travels to ribosome.

c)

Ribosome

Serine   Threonine   Aspartic acid

d)

protein

* note: uracil, not thymine, is attracted to adenine

Figure 26.

a) A segment of DNA separates from its complement and binds with RNA. b) The RNA breaks away as messenger RNA (mRNA) and moves to the cytoplasm. c) The mRNA attaches to a ribosome. There, small units of RNA known as transfer RNA (tRNA) carry specific amino acids to the mRNA. d) The amino acids join to form a protein, which is released. The mRNA is also released, and the ribosome can then bind with another mRNA molecule.

The tRNA consists of short strands of nucleotides that carry specific amino acids to the ribosomes (Figure 26c). There the amino acids are assembled and joined to form protein molecules. Once assembled, the protein, tRNA, and mRNA separate. The protein is then released and the mRNA leaves the ribosome (Figure 26d).

Sometimes a gene mutates. For example, a cosmic ray may delete a base from the normal sequence of bases in a segment of the DNA. The mRNA produced will then code for a different sequence of amino acids. The result will be a different protein. In rare cases, the new protein may be more beneficial than the old one. The organism will be better able to cope with the environment than other members of the species. In most cases, the new code will fail to produce a protein or it will produce one that is useless or harmful.

Experiment 5.3

A Three-Dimensional Model of DNA

Materials

✓ cardboard

✓ heavy wire

✓ scissors

✓ crayons or colored pens

✓ other appropriate materials

Using cardboard, heavy wire, scissors, crayons or colored pens, and any other materials that seem appropriate, build a partial model of the DNA molecule. Figure 23 provides useful information, but a three-dimensional model will provide a more realistic picture of the molecule.

Experiment 5.4

Gene Coding and a Mutation

Materials

✓ pencil

✓ notebook

✓ Figures 25 and 27

Figure 27 represents a short segment of DNA. Assume that the lower side is used to produce part of an mRNA molecule. What sequence of bases will be present in the mRNA created on this segment of the DNA? Remember, uracil (U), not thymine, bonds with adenine in RNA molecules. Record the base sequence in your notebook.

Next, using Figures 25 and 27, record the sequence of amino acids (reading from left to right) that tRNA will deliver to the mRNA on a ribosome. What is the significance of the last codon (it should be UAG) on the mRNA?

Suppose that a cosmic ray strikes and destroys the base pair at the extreme left-hand end of the DNA shown in Figure 27.

T	T	C	G	C	C	G	A	T		A	A	G	A	A	C	G	C	C	T	T	T	G	T	T	T	A	G
A	A	G	C	G	G	C	T	A		T	T	C	T	T	G	C	G	G	A	A	A	C	A	A	A	T	C

Figure 27.

This drawing represents a segment of a DNA molecule. Assume the lower strand is used to make mRNA. Remember: A = adenine; T = thymine; C = cytosine; and G = guanine. Also remember that in RNA, uracil (U), not thymine, bonds with adenine. What sequence of amino acids will the tRNA deliver?

What effect will it have on the protein that will be produced by the mRNA and tRNA?

Science Project Ideas

◆ The hemoglobin protein in the red blood cells of people with sickle-cell anemia differs from normal hemoglobin in just one of the more than 400 amino acids found in the molecule—valine is found where glutamic acid is normally located in the molecule. How can you account for this change?

◆ You know that some genes are dominant and others are recessive. Consider an organism that is heterozygous for some trait. How is the recessive gene repressed from coding during the formation of messenger RNA?

Experiment 5.5

A Model to Show How DNA Controls the Making of Proteins

Materials

- ✓ cardboard
- ✓ heavy wire
- ✓ scissors
- ✓ crayons or colored pens
- ✓ other appropriate materials

Build a three-dimensional model to show how mRNA is made. Then use the mRNA, together with a model of tRNA, to show how protein molecules are created in the cytoplasm of a cell.

Science Project Ideas

- ◆ Find out all you can about the Human Genome Project. What are the benefits of this project?

- ◆ What are marker genes and how are they used?

- ◆ What is recombinant DNA?

- ◆ What are transgenic animals?

- ◆ What is mitochondrial DNA? How is it used to study the evolution of humans?

DNA AND EVOLUTION

DNA provides strong evidence that we are descended from a common ancestor. Over time, DNA changes as a result of mutations and random errors in the duplication of DNA during mitosis and meiosis. We would expect that the differences in the DNA of species would be greater the greater the time since they diverged from a common ancestor. By knowing the average rate at which DNA changes, scientists can estimate the time that different species separated from a common ancestor.

Cytochrome c is an enzyme found in organisms as different as humans and yeast. The gene that codes for this enzyme has evolved since early life-forms appeared. As a result, the number of differences in the sequence of the nucleotide bases in the DNA can be used to find out how closely various species are related. Table 7 shows the number of differences in the sequence of bases between humans and several other organisms.

Since proteins are made by the coding in DNA, differences in common proteins can also be used to measure the degree of separation of different species. Red blood cells contain hemoglobin, which combines with oxygen. In one protein found in hemoglobin, chemists have analyzed the sequence of amino acids. When compared to humans, the sequence is identical for chimpanzees. It differs in 18 out of 141 amino

Table 7:

THE NUMBER OF DIFFERENCES IN THE SEQUENCE OF THE BASES IN THE GENE THAT CODES FOR CYTOCHROME C BETWEEN HUMANS AND OTHER SPECIES.

Organisms	Number of differences
humans and pigs (another mammal)	13
ducks (bird)	17
rattlesnake (reptile)	20
tuna (fish)	31
yeast (fungi)	66

acids for horses, 35 out of 141 for chickens, 62 out of 141 for newts (amphibian), and by 68 out of 141 for carp (a bony fish).

In Experiment 5.7 you can compare corresponding sections of primate DNA, but first you can compare the anatomy of primates.

Experiment 5.6

Primate Anatomy

Materials

✓ Figure 28

Darwinists believe that apes (gibbons, orangutans, chimpanzees, and gorillas) and humans are descendants of a common ancestor. Figure 28a shows the skeletons of apes and a human. What is similar about these skeletons? In what ways do they differ? Based on the skeletons, which ape would you conclude was last to break off from an ancestral line leading to humans? What makes you think so?

Comparisons of human and ape feet and skulls are shown in Figure 28b. In what ways are these skulls and feet similar? In what ways do they differ?

Science Project Idea

Observe apes in a zoo or on a video of a documentary about one or more of these animals. Record your observations. List the ways in which they act like humans. List, also, the ways in which they behave differently from humans.

a)

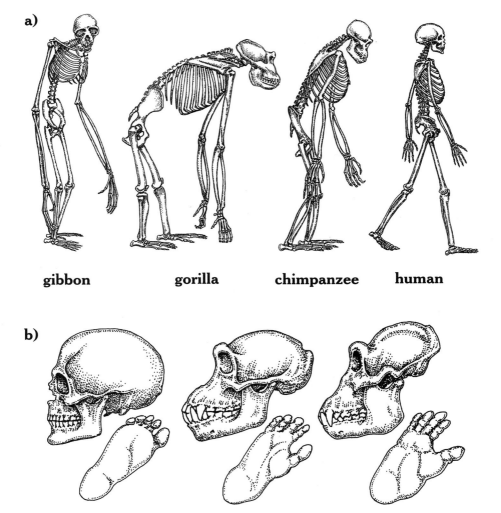

gibbon   **gorilla**   **chimpanzee**   **human**

b)

human   **chimpanzee**   **gorilla**

Figure 28.

a) The skeletons of apes and a human.
b) Human, chimpanzee, and gorilla skulls and feet.

Experiment 5.7

Primates and DNA

Materials

✓ cardboard
✓ shears
✓ ruler

✓ sticky notes, a stack of each of 4 colors (2 in × 2 in)

Today biochemists can compare sections of DNA in different species that code for certain proteins. In this experiment, you will prepare models of sections of DNA. The models will represent similar sections of the DNA from the African apes (gorillas and chimpanzees) and humans.

Prepare three pieces of cardboard, each one 60 cm (2 ft) by 5 cm (2 in). The cardboard pieces will represent one side of the DNA "ladder," which consists of deoxyribose and phosphate linked together. Use 2 inch by 2 inch sticky notes cut in half to represent the bases (thymine [T], guanine [G], adenine [A], and cytosine [C]) attached to one side of the DNA. Use different-colored sticky notes to represent the different bases. For instance, green sticky notes could represent guanine, red could represent adenine, yellow thymine, and orange cytosine. If all the sticky notes are of the same color, simply label them T, G, A, or C as shown in the sequences below. There is no need to model the other side of each DNA sequence because you know that adenine always joins with thymine and guanine is always paired with cytosine.

Prepare three hypothetical models of DNA strands with the following sequences of bases, starting from the left. Although hypothetical, these strands are similar to those found in the species whose names you will use to label them.

ATTAGCCAACCAAATACGGAGG (Human)
ATTAGCCAACCATTTCCGGAGG (Chimp)
ATTACCTAACCAAATCAGGCGG (Gorilla)

Compare the human and chimpanzee base sequences. In how many places do they differ? Repeat the process for human and gorilla sequences. In how many places do they differ? Based on this evidence, would you conclude that humans are more closely related to chimpanzees or to gorillas? Does this conclusion agree with your conclusion from the previous experiment?

Prepare a fourth model. In this model hypothesize what the corresponding DNA sequence may have looked like in a common ancestor to the apes and humans.

A comparison of all the DNA sequences in humans and chimpanzees reveals that 98.8 percent of human and chimpanzee DNA is identical. What percent of the sequences you examined are identical?

Appendix

SCIENCE SUPPLY COMPANIES

Carolina Biological Supply Company
2700 York Road
Burlington, NC 27215-3398
(800) 334-5551
http://www.carolina.com

Connecticut Valley Biological
Supply Company
82 Valley Road
P.O. Box 326
Southampton, MA 01073
(800) 628-7748
http://www.ctvalleybio.com

Delta Education
80 Northwest Boulevard
P.O. Box 3000
Nashua, NH 03061-3000
(800) 442-5444
http://www.delta-education.com

Edmund Scientifics
60 Pearce Avenue
Tonawanda, NY 14150-6711
(800) 728-6999
http://scientificsonline.com

Educational Innovations, Inc.
362 Main Avenue
Norwalk, CT 06851
(888) 912-7474
http://www.teachersource.com

Fisher Science Education
4500 Turnberry Drive
Hanover Park, IL 60133
(800) 955-1177
http://www.fisheredu.com

Frey Scientific
100 Paragon Parkway
Mansfield, OH 44903
(800) 225-3739
http://www.freyscientific.com/

NASCO-Fort Atkinson
901 Janesville Avenue
P.O. Box 901
Fort Atkinson, WI 53538-0901
(800) 558-9595
http://www.nascofa.com/

NASCO-Modesto
4825 Stoddard Road
P.O. Box 3837
Modesto, CA 95352-3837
(800) 558-9595
http://www.nascofa.com

Sargent-Welch/VWR Scientific
P.O. Box 5229
Buffalo Grove, IL 60089-5229
(800) 727-4386
http://www.sargentwelch.com

Science Kit & Boreal Laboratories
777 East Park Drive
P.O. Box 5003
Tonawanda, NY 14150
(800) 828-7777
http://sciencekit.com

Ward's Natural Science
P.O. Box 92912
Rochester, NY 14692-9012
(800) 962-2660
http://www.wardsci.com

Further Reading

Beatty, Richard. *Genetics*. Orlando, Fla.: Raintree Steck-Vaughn Publishers, 2001.

Bombaugh, Ruth. *Science Fair Success, Revised and Expanded*. Springfield, N.J.: Enslow Publishers, Inc., 1999.

Gardner, Robert. *Science Fair Projects—Planning, Presenting, Succeeding*. Springfield, N.J.: Enslow Publishers, Inc., 1998.

Holmes, Thom and Laurie. *Feathered Dinosaurs: The Origin of Birds*. Berkeley Heights, N.J.: Enslow Publishers, Inc., 2002.

Lawson, Kristan. *Darwin and Evolution for Kids: His Life and Ideas with 21 Activities*. Chicago: Chicago Review Press, Inc., 2003.

Walker, Richard. *Genes & DNA*. Boston: Kingfisher, 2003.

Wallace, Holly. *Classification*. Chicago: Heinemann Library, 2001.

Internet Addresses

The BBC Evolution Web site. <http://www.bbc.co.uk/education/darwin/index.shtml>.

In the Beginning Evolution for Children and Beginners. <http://www.information-entertainment.com/ScienceMath/Evolution.html>.

The PBS Evolution page. <http://www.pbs.org/wgbh/evolution/>.

Index